# GAMES
## for ALL SEASONS

**PLAY IN**

Fall

Winter

Spring

Summer

To our families for their love and encouragement.

Thanks Mom, Dad, Adlai Jr., Cody, Autumn, and Coral.

Thanks Dick, Kevin, Meghan and Cliff.

# GAMES for ALL SEASONS

By
**ALEXANDRA CLEVELAND** and
**BARBARA CATON**

Illustrations by
**JANET McDONNELL**

A **BUILDING BLOCKS** PUBLICATION

38W567 Brindlewood, Elgin, Illinois 60123

ART:

Cover and Text Illustrations                Janet McDonnell
                                            Arlington Heights, Illinois

Cover Graphics:                             David Van Delinder
                                            Studio IVV
                                            Elgin, Illinois

Text and Graphics Layout:                   Karen Wollscheid
                                            McHenry, Illinois

PUBLISHED BY:

38W567 Brindlewood
Elgin, Illinois 60123

DISTRIBUTED BY:

Gryphon House              Consortium Book Sales      Monarch Books
P.O. Box 207               1045 Westgate Drive        5000 Dufferin St., Unit K
Beltsville, MD 20704       St. Paul, MN 55114         Downsview, Ontario
                                                      Canada M3H 5T5

(Educational Stores        (U.S. Book Trade)          (All Canadian Orders)
 & Catalogs)

# Contents

# Contents

## WINTER

# Contents

## SPRING

# Contents

## SUMMER

# Play

# GAMES

## Help Children Learn SKILLS:

- **Gross Motor**

- **Fine Motor**

- **Math** ⇨

- **Language**

- **Social**

- **Creative**

# GAMES

## Are:

- **For Themes
  Seasons
  Holidays**

- **Original**

- **Easily Adapted**

- **Fun to Play**

- **Quick
  to Prepare**

# Climb the Apple Tree

## Themes

Fall

Apples

Trees

## Use With

Individuals

Pairs

## Skills

Eye-Hand
  Coordination

Visual Control

Cooperation

## Materials and Supplies

Long wrapping paper tubes

Red construction paper

Bulletin board putty

### Make Your APPLE TREE

1. Cut 3 or 4 apples for each apple tree.

2. Using putty, stick the apples near the tops of the paper tubes.

# Activity

### Playing With Individual Children

Hold the apple tree at the child's level. Starting at the bottom of the tube, have her "climb" the apple tree by alternating her hands one above the other until she reaches the top. When the child reaches the top, have her pick one apple, and give it to you. Encourage her to climb again and again until all the apples are gone.

### Playing With Pairs of Children

Using the smaller apple pattern, make 6-8 apples for each tube. Stick them at the top of each one.

Have the children "climb" the tree together by taking turns alternating their hands one above their partner's hand. When they reach the top, each child picks an apple, and gives them to you. Continue playing until all the apples are gone.

### Play Again – It's Fun!

*Climb the Color Tree:* Make color, number, shape, animal, etc. cards. Stick them at the top of the tube. Play as above, letting the child pick a card each time he climbs to the top. As he picks the card, have him tell you what color it is, name the letter, etc.

# Apple Picking

## Themes

Apples

Fall

Trees

## Use With

Individuals

## Skills

Body
  Coordination

Eye-Hand
  Coordination

## Materials and Supplies

Masking tape

Bulletin board putty

Bushel basket

Apples cut out of red, yellow, and/or green paper

## Activity

Tape the outline of a tree on the wall, making the top section high enough so the children have to stretch in order to reach the apples. Stick the apples on the top of the tree with the putty.

Have the children pick the apples one at a time and then squat down to put them in the basket.

### Play Again – It's Fun!

*Pick A Lemon:* Instead of picking apples from the tree, pick lemons, grapefruit, pineapples, colored fall leaves, etc.

Another time pick pine cones from an evergreen tree.

# Apple Fist Print

## Themes

Apples

Fall Colors

## Use With

Individuals

Small Groups

## Skills

Eye-Hand
  Coordination

Hand Strength

Play Together

## Materials

Green, yellow, red, and brown paint

Large sheets of white paper

## Activity

Have the children paint a large apple tree on butcher paper.

When the tree is dry, have them make apples by putting the bottom of their fists into the yellow or red paint and then stamping them on the tree. They can make stems on the apples by dipping their index fingers in brown paint and printing one above each apple.

**Play Again – It's Fun!**

*Apple Baskets:* Cut large bushel baskets out of brown paper and let the children stamp apples on them. Display the Apple Baskets near the apple tree.

# Johnny's Apple Tree

## Themes

Johnny
  Appleseed Day

Apples

Fall

Shapes

## Use With

Individuals

Small Groups

## Skills

Finger
  Coordination

Hand Strength

Parts/Whole

## Materials and Supplies

Red, yellow, and green clay or playdough

Several copies of the apple tree pattern sheet or one
  for each child

## Activity

Laminate or cover each apple tree with clear adhesive
paper.

When each child wants to play, give him some clay
and an apple tree. Have him pinch off small pieces of
clay, roll them into balls, and then put them on his
tree. After his tree is full of apples, have him press
and flatten each apple with his finger.

All done? Pick the apples off your tree and roll them
into one ball. Ready to play again!

18

# Johnny's Apple Tree

# Crumple and Paint Trees

## Themes

Fall Colors

Trees

## Use With

Individuals

Small Groups

## Skills

Hand Strength

Eye-Hand
 Coordination

Recognize
 Colors

## Materials and Supplies

Large sheets of paper

Full sheets of newspaper torn into 4 pieces

Yellow, orange, red, and brown poster paint

Small trim paint rollers

## Activity

Using small rollers, have the children paint a tree trunk and branches on their sheets of paper. While the trees are drying, let the children crumple pieces of newspaper into tight balls.

Using one ball for each color, have the children dip a ball into paint, and then dab it on the tree branches. When finished with that color, take another tight ball, dip it in a second color of paint and dab that color on the tree branches. Continue until the trees are full of fall color.

# Leaf Crush

## Themes

Leaves

5 Senses

Fall

## Use With

Individuals

Small Groups

## Skills

Hand Strength

Eye-Hand
 Coordination

Play Together

## Materials and Supplies

Tag board

Elmers® white glue

Dry brittle leaves of
 various colors

Paint brushes

## Activity

Cut out several large
leaf shapes from tag board. Thin down the glue with
water and pour small amounts into margarine tubs.

Have the children use paint brushes to spread glue
over the tag board leaves. (Cover each leaf entirely.)
Using both hands, have the children crush the
leaves, one or two at a time over the paper leaf. All
the pieces will fall on the glue. Continue crushing
leaves until the paper leaf is covered.

Let dry and hang around the room at the children's
eye level.

### Hint:

• Have the children touch the crushed leaves
 whenever they walk near them. How do they feel?
 Look for color.

# Colorful Trees

## Themes

Leaves

Fall

Colors

## Use With

Individuals

Small Groups

## Skills

Visual Control

Eye-Hand
 Coordination

Color Names

## Materials and Supplies

Large marbles

Large box lids

Small containers

Spoons

Yellow, red, orange, and brown tempera paint

### Make Your TREE SHAPES

1. Using the pattern on the next page as a guide, cut out large construction paper trees.

## Activity

Pour each color paint in a small container. Put a spoon and marble in each one. Set the supplies on the table.

When a child wants to make COLORFUL TREES, have her put a tree in a box lid. Use the spoon to scoop a marble into the lid. Roll the marble across and around the tree by tilting the lid from side-to-side and end-to-end. After she is done with the first color, encourage her to re-dip her marble or change colors. Continue rolling her different colored marbles around her tree until it is full of fall color.

### Play Again – It's Fun!

*Falling Snowflakes:* Use white and silver paint on blue colored paper.

*Pouring Rain:* Use gray and black paint on green construction paper.

22

# Colorful Trees

# Squirrel's Delight I

## Themes

Squirrels

Fall Nature

5 Senses

## Use With

Individuals

Small Groups

## Skills

Tactile
 Discrimination

Play Together

## Materials and Supplies

25 acorns

Tub filled with leaves

Small bushel basket or container

Several pairs of tongs

## Activity

Hide the acorns in the leaves. Let the child/ren find the acorns and put them in the bushel basket or container. After all the acorns have been found, let the child/ren put them back in the leaves. Then using tongs, pick them up one at a time and put them in the basket/container again.

**Play Again –
It's Fun!**

*Count the Acorns:* Draw 25 acorn size circles on a piece of posterboard. As the children find the acorns have them set each one inside a circle. When all the circles have been filled up, the players can point to and count the acorns with you.

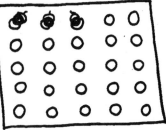

# Squirrel's Delight II

## Themes

Squirrels

5 Senses

Fall Nature

## Use With

Individuals

Small Groups

## Skills

Finger
  Coordination

Eye-Hand
  Coordination

One-to-One
  Correspondence

Count Objects

## Materials and Supplies

### Each Player Needs:

12 acorns (caps removed)

Large ball of soft dough

Empty egg carton with the lid cut off or an ice cube tray

Small plastic tray

## Activity

Hide the acorns by pressing them deep into the ball of soft dough. Put the dough and the egg carton on a plastic tray.

When a child wants to play, have her find the acorns by pinching off small pieces of dough with her index finger and thumb. Each time she finds one, have her put it in an empty egg carton section. She can keep track of how many acorns are left to find by counting the empty sections in the egg carton.

Let her help you hide the acorns, so the game is ready for her to play again or give to a friend.

# Fall Wipe-Offs

## Themes

Fall

## Use With

Individuals

Small Groups

## Skills

Eye-Hand Coordination

Finger Coordination

## Materials and Supplies

Large chalk board

Colored chalk

1" square wet sponge pieces

Small dish pan with water for rinsing the sponges

## Activity

Using colored chalk, draw large outlines of fall objects at the children's eye level (an apple, leaf, squirrel, pumpkin, acorn, rake, crow, straw hat). Each one should be 12" or larger.

When a child wants to play, have her choose a shape and stand in front of it. Give her a damp sponge and encourage her to erase the outline of the shape using small careful strokes. Encourage all the children to work slowly as they carefully erase the fall objects by following the lines.

### Play Again – It's Fun!

*Color By Color:* Use 2 or 3 colors of chalk to draw the outline of each fall object. Say to the player, *"First erase the red part of your leaf. Now erase the green part,"* etc. until the entire shape is erased.

# Fall Clean-Up

## Themes

Fall

## Use With

Small Groups

## Skills

Upper Body
 Control

Motor Planning

Play Together

## Materials and Supplies

Acorns, pine cones, and leaves

Scooter boards

Bushel basket

## Activity

Put the bushel basket in the center of a large open
area. Scatter the fall objects on the floor around the
basket.

Have each child lie on a scooter board, roll to a fall
object, and pick it up. Then roll to the bushel basket
and drop it in. Scoot away from the bushel basket
and pick up another object. Let everyone continue to
play until all the fall objects have been "cleaned-up."

# Fill the Pumpkin

## Materials and Supplies

Large brown grocery bag
Newspaper pages torn in half

## Activity

Set the grocery bag on the floor. Have the children use 2 hands to crumple each piece of newspaper into a tight ball. Toss the balls into the open bag until it is filled.

Tie the top of the bag closed, making a stem. Let the children paint and decorate their "pumpkin." Repeat the activity to make more "pumpkins."

### Continue to Play – It's Fun!

*Pass the Pumpkin:* Have the children sit in a circle. When the music begins, the children should start passing the pumpkin to each other. When the music stops, the child holding the pumpkin should hold it up high. Start the music again and continue passing it. (Using the large pumpkin for this game is great for building muscle strength and large muscle coordination.)

### Play Again – It's Fun!

*Fill the Small Pumpkin:* Have each child make his own pumpkin by using large lunch bags. Put everyone's pumpkins together to make a big pumpkin patch.

# Sticky Pumpkins

### Themes

Pumpkins

Fall

### Use With

Individuals

Small Groups

### Skills

Finger
  Coordination

Eye-Hand
  Coordination

## Materials and Supplies

Tag board or heavy paper

Clear Contact® paper

Large sheets of orange construction paper

### Make Your PUMPKIN FRAMES

1. Cut a large pumpkin shape
   out of the middle of each
   piece of heavy paper.

2. Stick the Contact® paper on
   the back of the shapes so the sticky sides are up.

## Activity

When a child/ren wants to play, give him a pumpkin
frame with the sticky side up and orange paper. Have
him tear the paper into small pieces and stick them
inside the pumpkin shape. Continue until the
pumpkin is completely orange.

### Play Again – It's Fun!

*More Fall Frames:* Cut out frames of leaves, turkeys,
squirrels, bats, etc. Back each with clear Contact®
paper. Let children choose the frames they want
along with colored construction paper.

*More Pumpkins:* Let the children tear orange
construction paper into small pieces and glue them
onto paper plates. They may want to add stems.

# Pumpkins in a Row

## Themes

Pumpkins

Shapes

## Use With

Individuals

Small Groups

## Skills

Eye-Hand
  Coordination

Hand
  Coordination

Matching

## Materials and Supplies

Orange soft dough

4"x11" strips of green paper

### Make Your STRIPS OF GREEN PAPER

1. Using a dark marker, draw 4 round pumpkins, ranging from small to large, on each strip.

2. **Optional:** Laminate or cover the strips with clear Contact® paper.

### OR

Draw the pumpkins on strips of orange posterboard or oilcloth instead of paper.

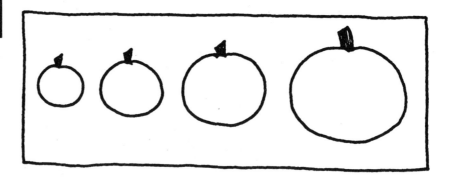

## Activity

Give each child a strip with the pumpkins drawn on it and a large ball of soft dough. Have the children make soft dough "pumpkins," trying to match them to the sizes of the circles on the strips. Set each "pumpkin" on the corresponding circle.

# Pass the Pumpkin

## Themes

Pumpkins

Fall

## Use With

Small Groups

Large Groups

## Skills

Position In
 Space

Pass Objects

Play Together

## Materials and Supplies

Small, real or inflated pumpkins

## Activity

Have the children stand, sit, or kneel in a circle, with every other child facing out. Give one child the pumpkin. When everyone starts singing PASS THE PUMPKIN, have the children begin to pass the pumpkin to each other while twisting at their waists. Whoever is holding the pumpkin when you sing the last line, should lay it down in front of him. When you start singing again, the child should pick up the pumpkin and begin passing.

**PASS THE PUMPKIN**

(tune: Row, Row, Row Your Boat)

*Pass, pass, pass the pumpkin*
*Pass it round and round.*

*Passing, passing, passing, passing,*
*Lay it on the ground.*

# Pumpkin Vine

## Themes

Pumpkins

Fall

Planting

Halloween

## Use With

Individuals

Small Groups

## Skills

Eye-Hand
Coordination

Finger and
Hand
Coordination

One-to-One
Correspondence

## Materials and Supplies

Orange soft dough

4-5 sheets of 8½"x11" orange paper

### Make Your PUMPKIN VINES

(See next page for example.)

1. On each sheet of orange paper, use a marker to draw a pumpkin vine.

2. Draw several small pumpkins on each branch.

## Activity

Give the children balls of soft dough and sheets of pumpkin vines. Have the children roll small dough "pumpkins" (about 1" in diameter) and put them, one at a time, on the vine.

After the vine is full of "pumpkins" have the children flatten each one by pressing it with their fingertips.

# Pumpkin Vine

# Pumpkin Roll

## Themes

Pumpkins

## Use With

Small Groups

## Skills

Body
Awareness

Body
Coordination

Encourage
Others

## Materials and Supplies

Tumbling mat

Small inflatable or plastic pumpkin

## Activity

Have one child lie down at one end of the mat with his legs together and his arms extended above his head. Put a pumpkin in his hands. Encourage him to maintain this position while he rolls down the mat. As he rolls have all the other players clap and cheer for him. When he's finished, give him a "Hi-5" for great effort.

# Pumpkin Planting

## Themes

Pumpkins

Seeds and Planting

## Use With

Individuals

Small Groups

## Skills

Eye-Hand Coordination

Finger Coordination

## Materials and Supplies

Pumpkin seeds in a margarine tub

Brown modeling clay

## Activity

Give the children balls of clay. Show them how to roll their clay into long hot dog shapes, thus making "rows for planting." Have the children each take a few pumpkin seeds and plant them, one at a time, by pushing each seed into the clay.

Encourage the children to start planting on the left side of the row and push each seed into the "soil" as deeply as possible. If a child needs more seeds, let him take them from the margarine tub. Set the "rows of seeds" in a sunny window.

### Play Again – It's Fun!

*Plant Real Seeds:*

1. Put damp paper towels along the sides of clear plastic glasses.

2. Slip a seed between the side of each glass and the paper towel.

3. Keep the towels damp.

4. Watch the seeds germinate. Later, plant them in dirt and watch them grow.

# Gigantic Spider Web

## Themes

Spiders, Bugs and Insects

Animal Homes

## Use With

Small Groups

Large Groups

## Skills

Motor Planning

Play Together

Taking Turns

## Materials and Supplies

Long piece of rope such as a clothesline or ball of very thick yarn

## Activity

Have the children stand in a large circle. Give the rope to one child. Let her be the first "spider." She gives the end of the rope to a child to hold. The "spider" continues to spin her web by unwinding the rope and giving it to a second child. While the first and second children hold their strands of the web, the "spider" continues to spin her web by going to a third child.

Change "spiders" several times as they continue to criss-cross the rope all around the circle to spin the web.

**Play With the Web – It's Fun!**

*Crawling In the Web:* Let the children, who are part of the web, take turns being the spider crawling over and under it.

*Look for Real Webs:* Show the children real webs that spiders have spun in your room, in trees, in flower beds, etc.

# Spin a Web

## Themes

Bugs and
 Insects

Spiders

Animal Homes

## Use With

Individuals

Small Groups

## Skills

Hand Strength

Eye-Hand
 Coordination

## Materials and Supplies

Heavy-duty paper plates

24" pieces of medium or heavy-weight yarn

Masking tape

Hand held hole punch

### Get Ready to SPIN YOUR SPIDER WEBS

1. Cut a large hole in the middle of each plate.
2. Wrap a short piece of masking tape around one end of each piece of yarn. This will make one end sturdy for weaving.

## Activity

Have the children punch holes around the inside edge of the paper plates. Encourage them to make their holes about 1"-2" apart. Tie the end of each child's piece of yarn to one hole. Let the children spin their spider webs by sewing the yarn through the holes, one at a time, going back and forth across their plates each time.

After each child finishes spinning his web, let him add bugs and spiders.

# Wacky Web

**Themes**

Spiders
Animal Homes

**Use With**

Small Groups

**Skills**

Eye-Hand
  Coordination

Visual Control

Play Together

## Materials and Supplies

Bingo markers

24"x36" sheets of paper

Black crayons

## Activity

Tape the sheet of giant paper to the wall at the children's level.

Have the children use bingo markers to daub large colored dots all over the paper. After they have finished daubing, let the children weave their WACKY WEB, by using black crayons to draw lines connecting all the dots.

When the WACKY WEB is all finished let the children draw or glue spiders on it.

**Play Again – It's Fun!**

(Especially appropriate for younger children.)

*Add the Spiders:* Draw simple webs on pieces of construction paper. (See next page for example.) Let the children use bingo markers to daub spiders on the lines of the web.

**Wacky Web**

# Spider Munchies

## Themes

Spiders, Bugs
and Insects

## Use With

Individuals

Small Groups

## Skills

Upper Body
Control

## Materials and Supplies

Lots of small plastic spiders, bugs and insects

Paper plates

Masking tape

Scooter boards

(draw web on
paper plate)

### Make the SPIDER WEB and PATH

1. In a large open area, make a
   20' long masking tape path.

2. At one end of the path put
   the "spider web" (paper
   plate).

3. Scatter the bugs on the floor along the length of
   the path.

## Activity

Let a child lie on a scooter board and pull himself
along the path to a bug. He picks up a bug and
scoots with it to the web. He puts it in the web and
then scoots back to get another bug and puts it in the
web. Continue until all the bugs have been caught in
the web.

### Hint:

- If more than one "spider" is catching bugs, make
  several different masking tape paths going to the
  web. Put bugs along each one.

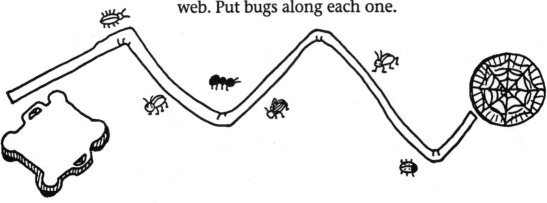

# Cat Creep

**Themes**

Pets

**Use With**

Individuals

Small Groups

**Skills**

Motor Planning

Visual Motor Control

## Materials and Supplies

Long piece of plain shelf paper, butcher paper, or for a more permanent game use a plastic runner

Wide black marker

### Make the CAT WALK

1. Draw cat's paw prints from one end of the paper/runner to the other. Use the illustration as a guide. Put the prints as close as necessary for your group of children.
2. Tape the CAT WALK to the floor of a less traveled area.

## Activity

Let the children do the CAT CREEP by walking on the paw prints with their hands and feet.

### Play Again – It's Fun!

*Puppy Paws:* Instead of using cat prints, use puppy paws. Let the children play the game with music. When the music starts, the first puppy walks down the path. When the music stops, he walks off the path and joins the puppies who are waiting to play. When the music starts again, the next puppy begins walking down the path. Continue, letting all the puppies have lots of turns to walk down the path.

# Follow the Flying Bat

## Themes

Bats

Night Creatures

Halloween

## Use With

Small Groups

Large Groups

## Skills

Eye-Hand
Coordination

Visual Tracking

## Materials and Supplies

Flashlight

## Activity

Have the children lie on their backs on the floor. Darken the room. Pretend that the light from the flashlight is a "bat." (Talk with the children about the fact that bats are animals who are awake at night and sleep during the day. Just the opposite of us.) Slowly move the "bat" across the ceiling. Have each child use his pointer finger to follow the "bat" as it flies around the sky.

### Hint:

- You could play music during this activity.

# I Spy an Owl

## Themes

Owls

Birds

Night Creatures

Halloween

## Use With

Small Groups

Large Groups

## Skills

Imagination

Visual Tracking

## Materials and Supplies

Flashlight

Toilet paper rolls (2 each child)

### Make YOUR BINOCULARS

1. Let the children glue/tape two toilet paper rolls together.

2. Decorate with colored markers if they want.

## Activity

Remind the children to bring their binoculars to the game. Have the children lie on their backs on the floor. Darken the room.

Tell the children that an owl is coming to visit them. Shine the light on the ceiling. Tell the children to look through their binoculars and find him. When they do, call out, *"I spy the owl."* Turn off the flashlight. Say, *"He disappeared. Let's keep looking for him."* Shine the light in another place. Encourage the children to look and call out. Repeat often.

After the game read OWL BABIES by Bill Waddel.

### Play Again – It's Fun!

*Follow the Owl:* Let the "owl" (light) slowly fly around the ceiling. Have the children track him with their binoculars.

# Bat Cave

## Themes

Bats

Animal Homes

Night Creatures

Halloween

## Use With

Individuals

Small Groups

## Skills

Upper Body
Control

Motor Planning

Eye-Hand
Coordination

## Materials and Supplies

Large bat cave cut from a piece of dark butcher paper
or posterboard

Lots of different sized bats (See patterns on the next
page.)

Scooter boards

Bulletin board putty

## Activity

Tape the BAT CAVE to one wall at the children's level.
Using bulletin board putty, stick the bats very low on
a different wall.

Have each child lie on her stomach on a scooter, pull
herself over to the wall and get a bat. Holding the
bat, have her pull herself over to the BAT CAVE and
stick the bat to the CAVE. Let the children continue
until all the bats have gathered in their BAT CAVE.

Let the children help you fly the bats out of their
cave to another wall. Stick them on that wall and
now everyone is ready to play BAT CAVE again.

**Play Again – It's Fun!**

*Put:*
- Spiders In a Web
- Birds In a Nest
- Bees In a Hive

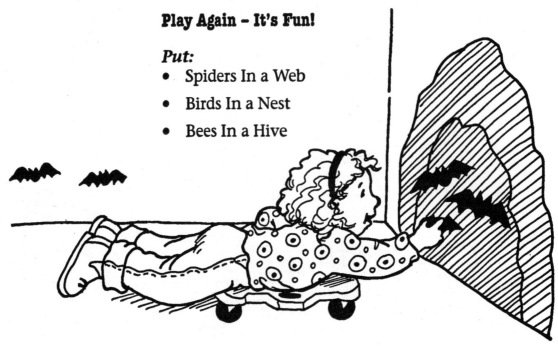

**Bat Cave**

# Bats at Night

## Themes

Bats

Night Creatures

Halloween

## Use With

Pairs of
  Children

## Skills

Visual Tracking

Eye-Hand
  Coordination

Cooperation

## Materials and Supplies

White crayons or chalk

Large sheets of black paper

Flashlight

## Activity

Tape the black paper to the table. Have the children work in pairs, one child with the flashlight and the other one with the crayon/chalk.

Have the child with the flashlight pretend it is a bat. Very slowly move the light around the paper, as if the bat was flying in the night. Have the child with the crayon/chalk follow the light, drawing the flight of the bat.

When the bat has landed, have the children draw or glue a bat on their paper at the end of the flight.

# Fall Match-Ups

## Themes

Fall

Halloween

## Use With

Small Groups

## Skills

Upper Body Control

Eye-Hand Coordination

Matching

## Materials and Supplies

4 or more small pictures of a bat, spider, owl, cat, pumpkin, jack-o-lantern, scarecrow, squirrel, and leaf. (Use pictures on the following pages or stickers with the backing paper left on them.)

At least 18 margarine tubs with lids

Scooter boards

### Make Your FALL MATCH-UPS

1. Duplicate the fall figures at least 4 times each. (More if there is a large group of children.) Color if you want.

2. Keep two sets of pictures for yourself.

3. Using the other two sets, put one figure, face up in each margarine tub.

## Activity

Scatter the tubs, which have pictures in them, on a large floor area. Mix up the other 2 sets of pictures and keep them in your hand. Have the players lie on scooter boards on their stomachs.

When you say *"Go"* have the players scoot to you. Give each one a picture. Have the children scoot from container to container looking for the pictures which match theirs. When a child finds a match he should drop the picture in the container and then scoot back to you for another picture. Continue playing until all the pictures have been matched.

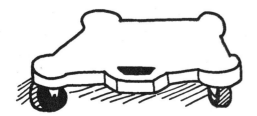

# Fall Match-Ups

**Fall Match-Ups**

# In the Cave

## Themes

Animal Homes

Bats

Spiders

Halloween

## Use With

Individuals

Small Groups

## Skills

Visual Control

Memory

## Materials and Supplies

Large appliance box or a table covered on two sides and one end with a dark sheet or paper (The children may want to paint it.)

Pictures of cave dwelling creatures – several of each (spiders, bats, bears, mice, lizards)

Flashlight

### Make Your CAVE

1. Enlarge and tape the pictures on the next page to the inside walls and ceiling of the box.

## Activity

Have the children crawl into the "cave," one at a time, and shine the flashlight on each picture. When the child comes out, have him tell you all the things he can remember seeing.

### Play Again – It's Fun!

*Circle What You Saw:* Have a sheet with pictures of the cave dwelling creatures on it. When a child comes out of the cave, have her look at the sheet and use her index finger to circle all the things she remembers seeing.

*How Many Spiders?* After a child tells you all the things he saw, ask him, *"Tell me, how many spiders did you see?"*

# In the Cave

# Shine a Shape

## Themes

Shapes

## Use With

Individuals

## Skills

Visual Motor Control

Eye-Hand Coordination

Recognize Shapes

## Materials and Supplies

Tape

Flashlight

Green and orange markers

### Make Your SHINE A SHAPE POSTERS

1. Get 3, 3'x3' sheets of paper. Draw a bold, giant triangle on one, circle on the second one, and square on the third one.

2. Draw a large dot in the corners of the triangle and square. (One dot should be green to show the children where to begin.)

3. Draw a series of large dots around the circle. (One dot should be green to show the children where to begin.)

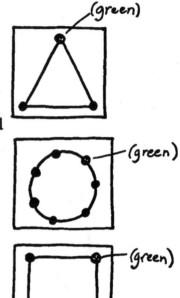

(green)

(green)

(green)

## Activity

Tape the SHINE A SHAPE posters to the wall at the children's eye level. When a child wants to play, give him a flashlight. Have him stand about 3' from the wall in front of the shape. (Put a piece of colored tape on the floor to show the children where to stand.)

Have him start by shining the light on the green dot and then moving clockwise along the line, stopping at each dot. When he finishes the first shape, encourage him to trace that shape again or move to the next one.

### Hint:

• For children just learning to trace or needing special reinforcement to draw their shapes, have 2 or 3 posters of the same shape on the wall.

# Thanksgiving Blueberry Pie

## Themes

Foods

Thanksgiving

## Use With

Individuals

Small Groups

## Skills

Hand and
  Finger
  Coordination

Finger Strength

Count Objects

Parts/Whole

## Materials and Supplies

Blue soft dough or modeling clay

Small aluminum pie pans (tart or pot pie size)

## Activity

When a child wants to make a BLUEBERRY PIE, give him a ball of dough/clay and a pie pan. Let him fill his pan with lots of blueberries by pinching off small pieces of blue dough/clay, rolling them in balls, and putting them in his pan. Continue until the pie pan is full.

After filling the pan with "blueberries" encourage the child take them out one at a time. Count them with the child as he does. Squish the "blueberries" back into one big ball. Now you're ready to make another pie. Delicious!

**Play Again – It's Fun!**

**More Pies:** Use different colored dough/clay to make a variety of pies. For example:

- Red dough/clay – Strawberry/Cherry pie
- Yellow dough/clay – Lemon pie
- Brown dough/clay – Chocolate pie

# Turkey Feather Fun

## Themes

Turkeys

Feathers

Thanksgiving

## Use With

Individuals

Small Groups

## Skills

Visual Control

Upper Body
 Control

Self Esteem

## Materials and Supplies

Modeling clay

Small colored feathers

## Activity

Have each child make a turkey's body by rolling a
wad of clay into a ball. Set the clay on the floor. Let
the children pick feathers and blow them across the
floor/table to their balls of clay. Have the children
stick their feathers, one at a time, into the clay.

Repeat with as many feathers as each child would
like. Some children might want to put heads on their
turkeys with cut-up toilet paper rolls, collage
materials, or construction paper.

### Hint:

* Let the children take their turkeys home and use
 for a table decoration.

### Play Again – It's Fun!

*Blow the Feathers:* Let the children use empty
squeeze bottles to blow their feathers across the
floor/table.

# Turkey In the Bag

## Themes

Thanksgiving

Turkeys

## Use With

Individuals

Small Groups

## Skills

Hand Strength

Eye-Hand
 Coordination

Cooperation

## Materials and Supplies

Large brown grocery bag

Newspaper pages torn in half

## Activity

Set the newspaper pieces on a table. Open the grocery bag and set it on the floor nearby.

Have the children use 2 hands to crumple each piece of newspaper into a tight ball. Toss the balls into the bag. Continue until the bag is full.

Tie the top of the bag closed. Turn it on its side and add a paper turkey head to the end which is tied. Have the children cut out or tear colored paper feathers and glue them on the other end of the turkey.

**Play Again – It's Fun!**

*Small Turkeys In the Bag:* Have the children make individual turkeys using large brown lunch bags.

# Turkey Target

## Themes

Turkeys

Thanksgiving

## Use With

Individuals

Small Groups

## Skills

Visual Control

Eye-Hand Coordination

## Materials and Supplies

Socks rolled into balls or beanbags set in a pail

Large box

### Make Your TURKEY TARGET

1. Set the box lengthwise on its side. Put a paper turkey head on one end and lots of colored feathers at the other end.

2. Cut a large hole in one or two sides of the turkey.

## Activity

Place the TURKEY TARGET in an open area. Set the pail of socks/beanbags near the turkey. Have the children lie on their tummies and throw socks/beanbags, one at a time, through the hole in the turkey. After he's all "stuffed," take out the socks/beanbags and play again.

# Turkey Tickle

### Themes

Turkeys

Thanksgiving

5 Senses

### Use With

Pairs of
  Children

### Skills

Body
  Awareness

Tactile
  Awareness

Taking Turns

## Materials and Supplies

Feathers

## Activity

Working in pairs have one child take off his shoes and socks and roll up his sleeves and pant legs a little bit. Then close his eyes. The other child has the feather. He tickles his partner on any exposed skin. The child being tickled should either point to or name where he is being touched by the feather. Switch and play again.

### Hint:

- This is a great activity for parent volunteers to help with.

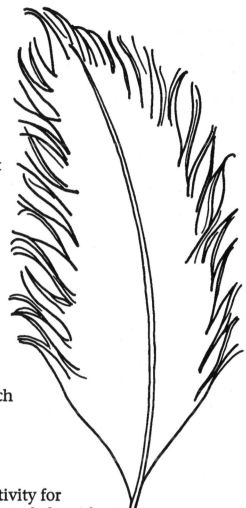

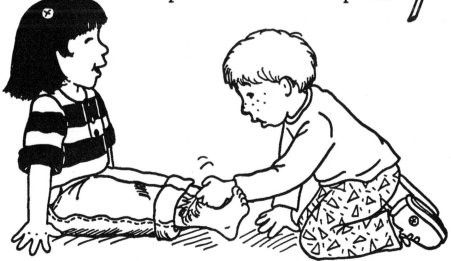

# Turkey Feathers

## Themes

Turkeys
Thanksgiving
Colors

## Use With

Individuals
Small Groups

## Skills

Visual Motor
Control
Finger
Coordination
Eye-Hand
Coordination
Color Names

## Materials and Supplies

Variety of colors of finger paints in shallow
containers

Fingerpaint paper

### Make TURKEY BODIES

(Children and/or adults can do this.)

1. Cut brown construction paper turkey heads. (See pattern on next page.)
2. Glue each turkey head to a piece of fingerpaint paper.
3. Draw a large ring around the turkey heads. (See illustration.)

## Activity

Have a child lay his turkey on the table. Let him give his turkey feathers by dipping the fingertips of one hand in one color of paint and then, starting at the turkey's body, drag his fingertips across the paper away from the body. Encourage the children to paint as many feathers and use as many colors as each would like.

### Play Again – It's Fun!

*Big Turkeys:* Have the children work in small groups on large turkeys.

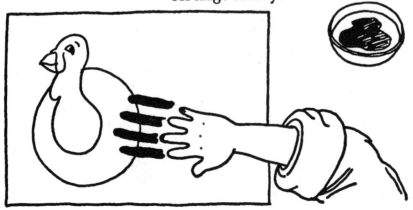

**Turkey Feathers**

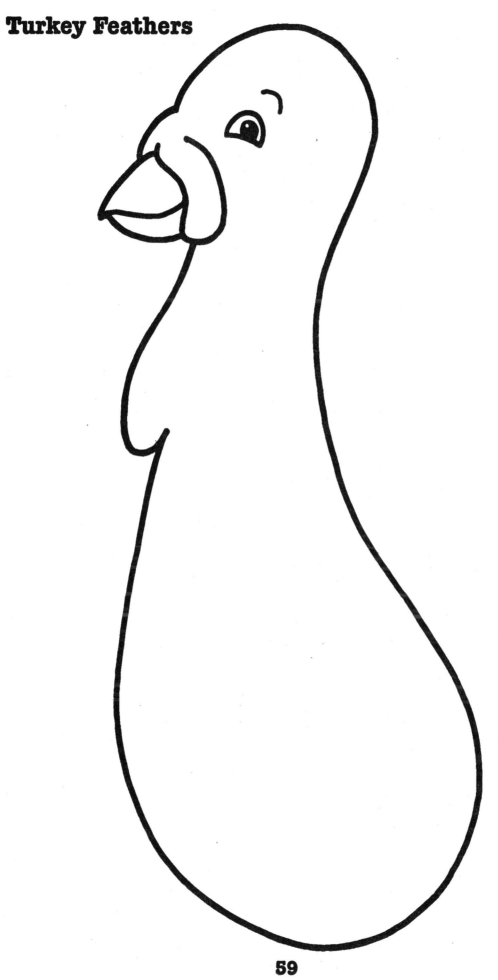

# Turkey Farm

## Materials and Supplies

Shallow amounts of brown paint in small containers

½" to 1" wide flat brushes

### Make Your BARNYARD

1. On a large sheet of butcher paper draw a barnyard including a large barn and a fence. (See illustration.)

## Activity

Hang the barnyard on an empty wall close to the floor.

Have the children kneel or sit in front of the barnyard. Give each of them a container of paint and a brush. Let them make TURKEYS for the farm by painting the underside of one of their hands (palms and fingers) and then pressing it firmly in the barnyard. Encourage the children to make as many turkeys as each would like.

### Play Again – It's Fun!

*Wild Turkey Farm:* Make wild turkeys by letting the children paint each finger a different color (red, purple, green, yellow, orange, etc.).

# Turkey Farm

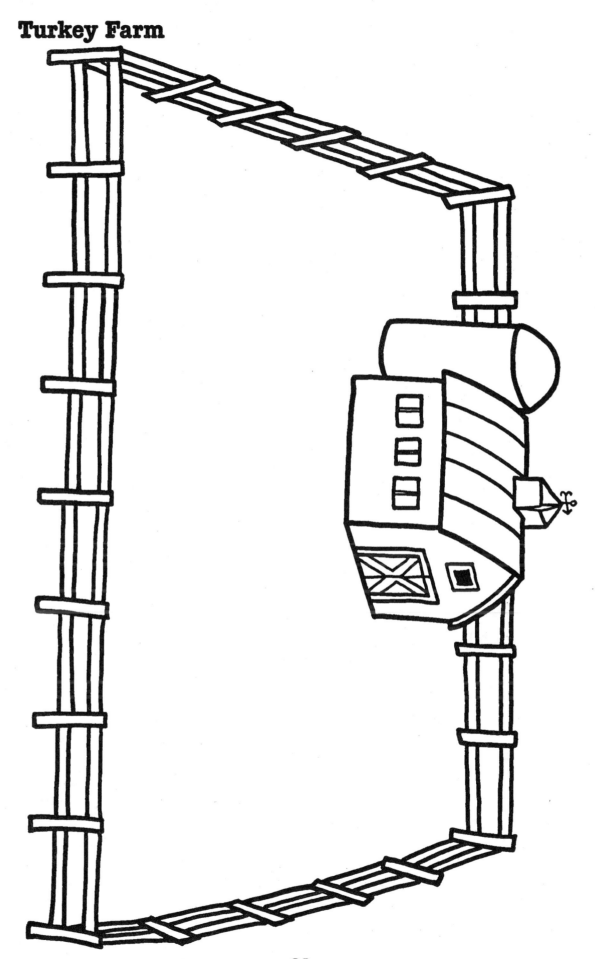

# Tape Tails

## Themes

Turkeys
Thanksgiving
Colors

## Use With

Individuals
Small Groups

## Skills

Hand and
  Finger
  Coordination

Eye-Hand
  Coordination

## Materials and Supplies

Rolls of ½" masking tape

Turkey pages (See next page.)

Crayons and/or washable markers

## Activity

Have the turkey pages, rolls of tape, and crayons/markers on the table.

Let the children put tail feathers on their turkeys. Have them tear off lengths of tape and stick them on the paper where they want the feathers to be. When finished, the children can use markers and/or crayons to color all the turkey feathers.

**Play Again – It's Fun!**

*Colored Tape Turkey Tails:* Use colored masking tape to make lots of turkey feathers.

**Tape Tails**

# Sail the Mayflower

## Themes

Oceans

Boats and Ships

Food

Thanksgiving

## Use With

Small Groups

Large Groups

## Skills

Body
  Coordination

Motor Planning

Body Strength

Taking Turns

## Materials and Supplies

Cardboard boxes big enough for a child to comfortably sit in (can also use scooters)

Provisions such as:

Pillows                    Blankets
Stuffed animals            Empty food boxes

## Activity

Put Mayflower Ships in a large open area (ocean). Let children pretend they are sailing across the ocean by having one child get in the "Mayflower" and 2 children push him across the "ocean." Switch and continue sailing.

### Hint:

- With a large group have several "Mayflowers" so more children can participate at one time.

**Play Again – It's Fun!**

*Take Provisions:* Have all the provisions on a shelf near the "Mayflowers." Let the children decide what they want to put in the "Mayflower" and then load it. Push it across the ocean.

# Plant the Corn

## Themes

Corn
Vegetables
Farm
Thanksgiving

## Use With

Individuals
Small Groups

## Skills

Finger
  Coordination
Eye-Hand
  Coordination

## Materials and Supplies

Ears of dried corn

Lots of 3"x12" strips of brown construction paper

Glue or Double-stick tape

Tweezers

## Activity

Have the children use their fingers to remove the corn kernels from the cobs. As each child finishes, give him a strip of construction paper. Help him squiggle a line of glue down the center of the strip or stick a piece of double-stick tape down the middle.

Let the children pretend to be farmers and PLANT THE CORN by picking up one kernel at a time with tweezers or their thumb and index finger and place it on the glue/tape. Continue until the fields are planted.

# Colored Corn

## Materials and Supplies

Watercolor paint trays

Small containers of water

Yellow construction paper

### Make Your CORN COBS

1. Using the pattern on the next page, cut out lots of corn cob shapes.

## Activity

Have the paint, water, and cobs on the table.

Show the children how to wet the fingertips on one hand and then press them into 4 different colors of paint, one fingertip in each color, such as red, yellow, orange, and brown. Have them press their fingertips on the CORN COB cut-out. Continue until the CORN COBS are "full of colored kernels."

You can add husks by:

- Gluing green pieces of construction paper to the cobs.
- Gluing real husks to the painted cobs.

### Play Again – It's Fun!

*More Colored Corn:* Make the corn kernels by dipping the end of pencil eraser in paint and then dabbing it on the CORN COB cut-out. Add husks if you want.

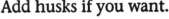

**Colored Corn**

# Dress Raggedy Ann and Andy

## Materials and Supplies

Large Raggedy Ann and/or Andy dolls

Raggedy Ann and Andy Dress-Up Cards

Variety of toddler size clothes, such as several:

Coats
Mittens
Boots
Hats
Scarves
Ear muffs

### Make Your RAGGEDY ANN and ANDY DRESS-UP CARDS

1. Duplicate each CARD once and color the 3 pieces of winter clothing on each one. (See pages 72-75.)

2. Cut them out and glue each CARD on a piece of construction paper.

3. Laminate or cover the CARDS with clear Contact® paper.

# Activity

1. Have the Raggedy Ann and/or Andy dolls.

2. Spread the winter toddler-size clothes on the floor.

3. Hold the DRESS-UP CARDS, picture side down.

Have a child pick a card, study it, and give it back to you. Have him look at all the clothes and pick up the 3 pieces he saw Raggedy Ann or Andy wearing. Let him dress one of the dolls. (Show the card to the child again if he needs help remembering which clothes were pictured.) As he is dressing his doll, let another child start playing.

After a child has dressed his doll, let him show the other children the "winter outfit." He might like to point to each article of clothing and everyone call out what it is. Let him undress his doll and put the clothes back on the floor.

## Hint:

• If you have more than 3-4 players, have several children dressing their dolls at the same time.

**Play Again – It's Fun!**

**Dress Yourself:** Instead of using dolls and toddler size clothes, use some of your children's winter clothes. Lay the clothes on the floor. Have a child pull a DRESS-UP CARD, look at what Raggedy Ann/Andy is wearing, then dress herself in the same clothes.

After she is dressed, let her model her "winter outfit" for the others. (Great activity for learning how to put on and take off winter clothes.)

# Raggedy Ann and Andy DRESS UP CARD

**Raggedy Ann and Andy DRESS UP CARD**

# Raggedy Ann and Andy DRESS UP CARD

# Raggedy Ann and Andy DRESS UP CARD

# Mitten Match-Ups

## Themes

Winter

Winter Clothes

Mittens

## Use With

Individuals

Small Groups

## Skills

Eye-Hand
Coordination

Finger
Coordination

Matching

## Materials and Supplies

Clothesline

Spring-loaded
clothes pins

Variety of mittens
and gloves

## Activity

String the clothesline, at the children's height, in a less traveled area of the room. Put the mittens/gloves and clothes pins in a basket. Set the basket near the clothesline.

Encourage the children to find matching pairs of mittens/gloves and hang them on the clothesline with the clothes pins. Continue until all the pairs are matched and hung.

### Play Again – It's Fun!

*Wallpaper Mittens Match-Up:* Using different wallpaper designs, cut pairs of wallpaper mittens and gloves. Put them, along with clothes pins, in a basket. Let the children pair the wallpaper mittens and gloves and hang them on the clothesline.

# Mitten Search

## Themes

Winter
Winter Clothes
Mittens

## Use With

Small and Large
  Groups

## Skills

Motor Planning
Matching
Cooperation
Play Together

## Materials and Supplies

Large thin blanket or a sheet

Enough pairs of mittens and gloves for each child

## Activity

Put one mitten from each pair on the floor. Cover the mittens with the blanket/ sheet. Keep the mates in a container.

Have the children sit cross-legged around the blanket/sheet and hold onto the edges with both hands. Hold up one mitten. Have the children raise the blanket/sheet a little. Name one child. Have him crawl under the blanket/sheet and find the matching mitten. Let him crawl out with the mitten, walk over to you and get the mate. Put on both mittens while continuing to play.

### Play Again – It's Fun

*Animal Search:* Have pairs of baby and adult animals such as dog and puppy, cat and kitten, cow and calf, horse and foal, pig and piglet, etc.. Put the babies under the blanket/sheet. Have the adults in a "barn." Hold up one adult animal. Name a child. Let her crawl under the blanket/sheet and find the baby. Give it to you.

# Winter Hang-Ups

## Themes

Winter
Winter Clothes

## Use With

Individuals

## Skills

Finger
  Coordination

Eye-Hand
  Coordination

Sequencing
  Sizes

## Materials and Supplies

Clothesline

Spring-loaded clothes pins

Wallpaper or construction paper hats, coats, mittens, and boots

### Make Your WINTER CLOTHES

1. Enlarge the patterns on the next page. Use them to make several graduated sets of hats, coats, mittens, and boots.

2. Laminate or cover the pieces with clear Contact® paper.

3. Put each set in a small clear bag or container.

## Activity

String the clothesline, in a less traveled area of the room, at the children's height. Have a basket of clothes pins and the "winter clothes" nearby.

Have each child or pair of children choose one set of "clothes" and put them in order from small to large on the floor by the clothesline. Use clothes pins to hang the clothes.

# Winter Hang-Ups

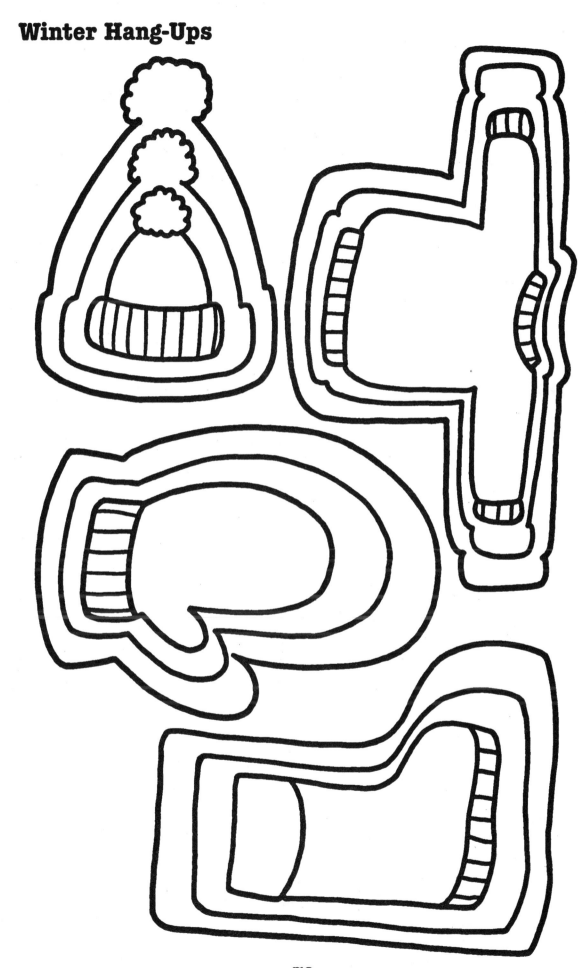

# Finger Foil Fun

## Themes

Winter

5 Senses

Any Theme or
  Season

## Use With

Individuals

Small Groups

## Skills

Finger
  Coordination

Eye-Hand
  Coordination

## Materials and Supplies

Tagboard or posterboard

Small containers of white glue

Heavy-duty aluminum foil

Winter shape pages (See patterns on pages 82-83)

### Make Your WINTER SHAPE PAGES

1. Enlarge the winter shapes on pages 82-83.
2. Duplicate several of each one.

## Activity *(3 day activity)*

### Day 1

Have the WINTER SHAPE PAGES and bottles of glue
on the table. Have each child choose a winter shape
and slowly follow the lines of the shape with glue.
Continue until all the lines have been covered. Put
the pages in a quiet area to dry.

### Day 2

Repeat step one, adding a second layer
of glue to the winter shape. Let dry
overnight.

### Day 3

Have the winter shapes and
aluminum foil on the table. Help each
child cut a piece of foil to cover her
shape. Lay the foil on top of the shape
and securely tape it around the edges.
Have the children use their index
fingers to rub over the foil covering
their shapes. Continue until the
outline of the winter shape appears.

## Play Again – It's Fun!

*Create Your Own Design*: Instead of having specific shapes, let the children create their own designs and shapes by drizzling glue on blank posterboard or tagboard.

*Color Your Shape:* After the children have "rubbed" their shapes through the foil, put colored markers on the table. Encourage the children to color their shapes and designs.

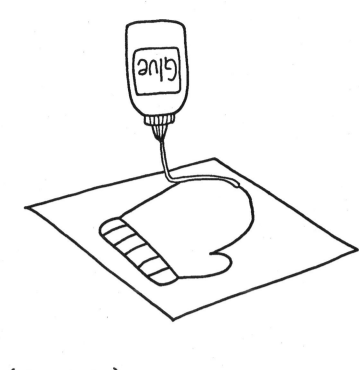

(aluminum foil)

**Finger Foil Fun**

# Finger Foil Fun

# Big Boots In the Snow

## Themes

Winter

Snow

## Use With

Individuals

Small Groups

## Skills

Motor Planning

Visual Motor Control

## Materials and Supplies

3-4 pairs of adult boots

Wide white tape/long clothesline (maybe tie 2 together)

## Activity

In a large, open area such as a gym or hallway, make a tape/rope path that winds, criss-crosses, and zig-zags around the area and returns to the beginning.

Have several pairs of boots at the beginning of the path. Let the children put them on and walk along the snowy path.

### Play Again – It's Fun!

*Obstacle Course:* Get several large white balls and boxes. Put them along the path. When children get to the "giant snowballs, tunnels, and boulders" let them decide how they want to move around, over, or through them.

# Fingertip Footprints

## Themes

Winter

Body
 Awareness

Self Concept

## Use With

Individuals

Small Groups

## Skills

Finger
 Coordination

Eye-Hand
 Coordination

## Materials and Supplies

Shallow amounts of black poster paint in small
 containers

3"x36" pieces of white paper – long pieces of wide
 adding machine tape

Half sheets of construction paper

Crayons and/or markers

## Activity

Give each child a long piece of paper and a container
of black paint. (Tape the paper to the table if
necessary.) Have the children make "footprints" by
dipping the index and middle fingers of one hand
into the paint and then "walking" them along the
paper to the other end. Have the children draw and
cut out pictures of themselves to glue at the end of
the paths.

**Hint:**

• Children will need to frequently re-dip their
 fingertips into the paint to keep their footprints
 dark.

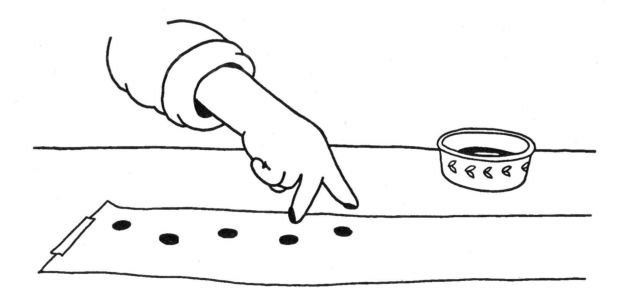

# Fingertip Snowflakes

## Themes

Winter

Snow

## Use With

Individuals

Small Groups

## Skills

Finger
Coordination

Eye-Hand
Coordination

Imagination

## Materials and Supplies

White poster paint in
small containers

8½"x14" light blue
construction paper

Crayons and/or
markers

## Activity

Have the children use the crayons and markers to draw snow scenes. When each child has finished, give her a container of white paint. Let her make snowflakes all over her picture by dipping one fingertip at a time into the paint and pressing it on the paper. Encourage the children to use all the fingertips on both hands – but remember, one at a time.

### Play Again – It's Fun!

*Fingertip Raindrops:*
Pour shallow amounts
of gray poster paint
into small containers.

Have the children draw windy spring pictures on construction paper. Encourage the children to add raindrops to their pictures, by dipping their fingertips into the gray paint and pressing them on the paper.

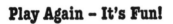

# Bottle Snowpals

## Themes

Snow

Winter Fun

Snow Families

## Use With

Individuals

Small Groups

## Skills

Eye-Hand
Coordination

Finger
Coordination

## Materials and Supplies

White packing peanuts

Small clear plastic soda
bottles (at least one
for each child)

White construction
paper circles

Collage materials

Glue

## Activity

Put the container of
styrofoam peanuts on
the table. Set the soda
bottles nearby. As the
children want to do
the activity, give them
each a bottle. Have
the children break the
packing peanuts in
half and put each half
in their bottle.
Continue until the
bottles are full. Have
each child put the cap
back on his bottle.

Now the children can
complete their snowpals
by using the white
circles for snowpal faces,
and collage materials for
clothes and features,
such as scarves, hats,
buttons, etc.

# Snowball Maze

## Themes

Winter

Toys

## Use With

Pairs

Small Groups

## Skills

Visual Motor Control

Cooperation

## Materials and Supplies

Ping pong balls

Box lid approximately 12"x18" or larger

## Activity

Cut one or more holes in the bottom of the lid, each one large enough for a ping pong ball to drop through.

Have 2 children stand and hold onto opposite ends of the lid. Place a ping pong ball in it. Encourage the children to work together to roll the ball from one end to the other end, from side to side, and all around, by tilting the lid and avoiding the holes.

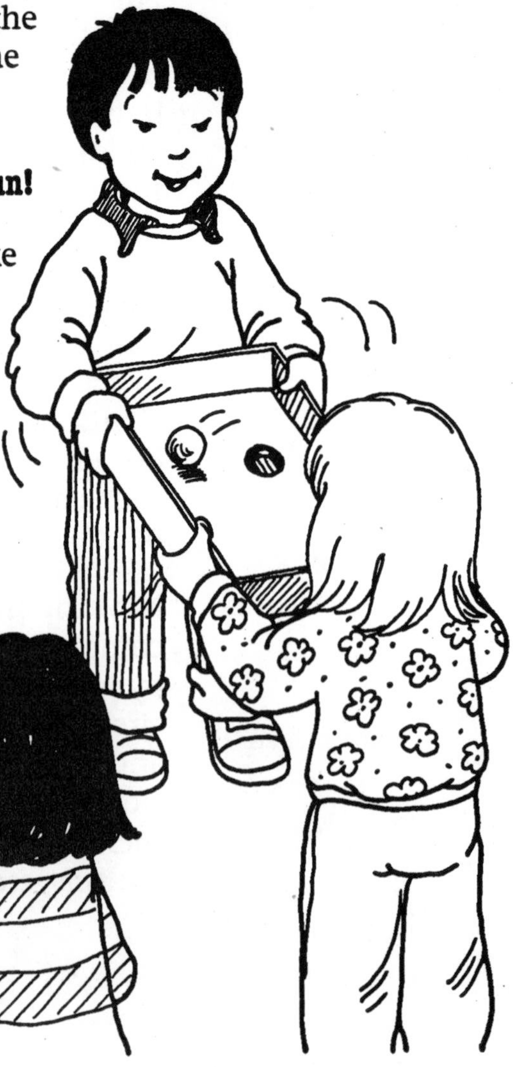

**Play Again – It's Fun!**

*Marble Maze:* Make smaller holes in the box lid and use large marbles or ball bearings.

To make this more challenging, cut several more holes in the lid.

# Snow Scene Bags

## Themes

Winter
Snow
Weather

## Use With

Individuals
Small Groups

## Skills

Visual Control
Hand Strength

## Materials and Supplies

Hand held hole punches

Small containers such as margarine tubs

Heavy-duty small recloseable plastic bags (sandwich bags)

Small pitcher of blue water

2"x6" strips of clear acetate (old theme folders), heavy-duty aluminum foil, and waxed paper

## Activity

Put the materials on a tray and set it on a table.

Have each child punch as many "snowflakes" as he would like out of the clear acetate, waxed paper and aluminum foil. After punching his "snowflakes," put them in a sandwich bag. Help him fill his bag about half full of blue water. Release as much air from the bag as possible and then seal it. (Tape closed for additional security.)

Encourage the children to tip, turn, and rotate their SNOW SCENE BAGS. Watch the movement of the "snowflakes."

### Play Again – It's Fun!

*More Snow Scenes:* Get a variety of small plastic snowflakes, snow pals, and other winter shapes. Let the children choose what shapes they want in their SNOW SCENES. Have them put one shape at a time in their bags. Add blue water, close, and play.

# Cotton Ball Snowpal

## Themes

Winter

Snow

Snowpals

## Use With

Individuals

Small Groups

## Skills

Eye-Hand
Coordination

Finger Strength

## Materials and Supplies

Cotton balls

Glue

Snowpal shapes

Tweezers and/or spring-loaded clothes pins

## Activity

Have all the supplies on the table. As each child wants to play, let him pick which snowpal shape he would like. Let him use a pair of tweezers to pick up one cotton ball at a time, dip it in the glue, and then place it on the snowpal's body. Continue until the snowpal is filled with fluffy snow.

### Hint:

- Children might want to use colored cotton balls to add buttons, facial features and other detail to their snowpals.

### Play Again – It's Fun!

*Snow Storm:* Tape a large travel poster of a snow scene to the table – building a snowpal, snow skiing, ice skating, etc. Let the children use tweezers to add as much cotton ball snow to the scene as they would like.

# Cotton Ball Snowpal

# Cotton Ball Snowpal

# Cotton Ball Snowpal

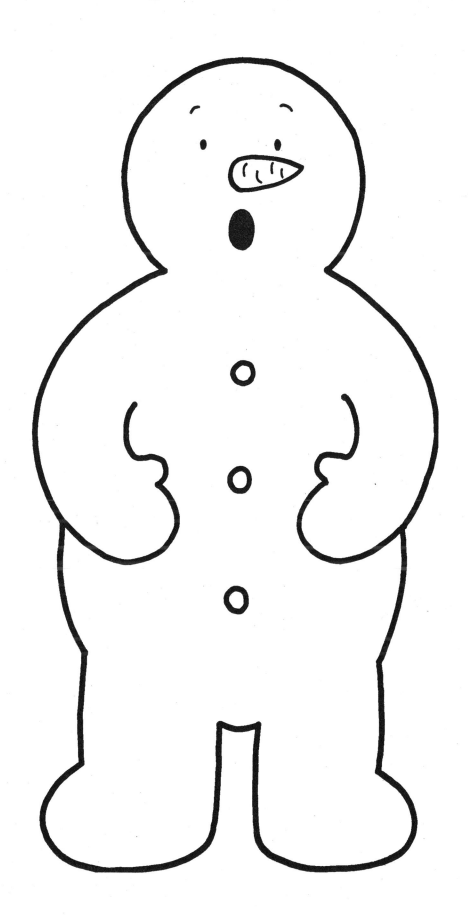

# Snowball Freeze

## Themes

Snow

Winter

## Use With

Large Groups

## Skills

Body
 Coordination

Motor Planning

Visual Motor
 Control

Follow
 Directions

Play Together

## Materials and Supplies

Several different size white styrofoam balls, white
 tennis balls, or sponge balls

FROSTY THE SNOWMAN music

## Activity

Have the children stand in a line approximately one
foot apart. (Maybe 5-6 children in each line.) Give
the first child in each line a snowball. Call out how

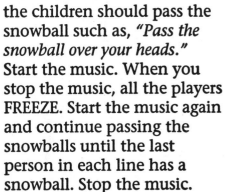

the children should pass the
snowball such as, *"Pass the
snowball over your heads."*
Start the music. When you
stop the music, all the players
FREEZE. Start the music again
and continue passing the
snowballs until the last
person in each line has a
snowball. Stop the music.

All the players with snowballs
walk to the front of their
lines. Give another direction
such as *"Pass the snowball
through your legs."* Start the
music and play. Keep playing
– it's fun!

### Here are a few commands to begin with:

- *"Pass the snowball over your
 heads. GO!"*

- *"Pass the snowball through
 your legs. GO!"*

- *"Pass the snowball over –
 under – over – under ... GO!*

- *"Twist – turn – and pass.
 GO!"*

# Ice Fishing

## Themes

Winter
Ice
Water Animals

## Use With

Individuals
Small Groups

## Skills

Eye-Hand
Coordination

Visual Motor
Control

Count Objects

## Materials and Supplies

3 or more ice cube trays

Several sheets of different colored acetate (old theme folders)

2 small fish buckets (medium size pails)

Small fish nets

### Make Your FISH

1. Cut out 36 small colored fish – small enough to fit in ice cube sections.

2. Put one fish cut-out in each ice cube section.

3. Fill the trays with water and freeze.

## Activity

Fill the water table or large tub half full of cold water. Add the ice cube fish.

Have the children go ICE FISHING by scooping the fish out of the water with their fish nets one at a time. Put each fish in the bucket. As the children are fishing, encourage them to count how many fish they have caught and how many are still in the water.

# Straw Snowflakes

## Themes

Winter

Snow

## Use With

Individuals

Small Groups

## Skills

Visual Control

Eye-Hand Coordination

Visual Motor Control

Matching

## Materials and Supplies

Straws

Small containers

Snowflake designs

### Make Your SNOWFLAKE DESIGNS

1. Duplicate the SNOWFLAKE DESIGNS on the next several pages.

2. Laminate or cover each one with clear Contact® paper.

3. Cut the straws into 4 different lengths and put them in separate containers:

   - 1 inch
   - 2 inches
   - 3 inches
   - 4 inches

## Activity

Put the SNOWFLAKE DESIGNS and containers of straws on the table. Let each child choose the SNOWFLAKE DESIGN she would like. Have her place appropriate length straws on the lines of the snowflake.

### Play Again – It's Fun!

*More Snowflakes:* Make lots of SNOWFLAKE DESIGNS. Do not laminate them. Let the children glue the straws to the DESIGNS and take them home when dry.

# Straw Snowflakes

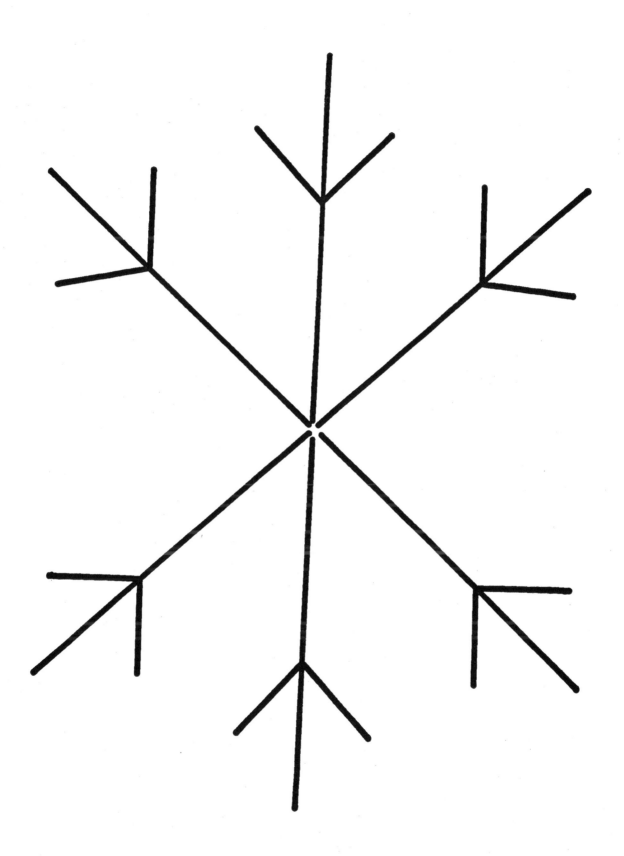

# Straw Snowflakes

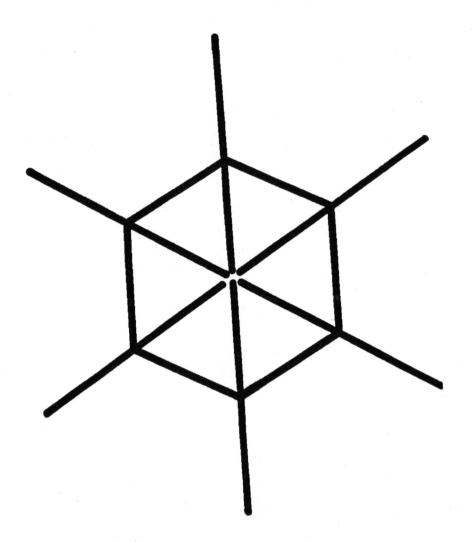

# Straw Snowflakes

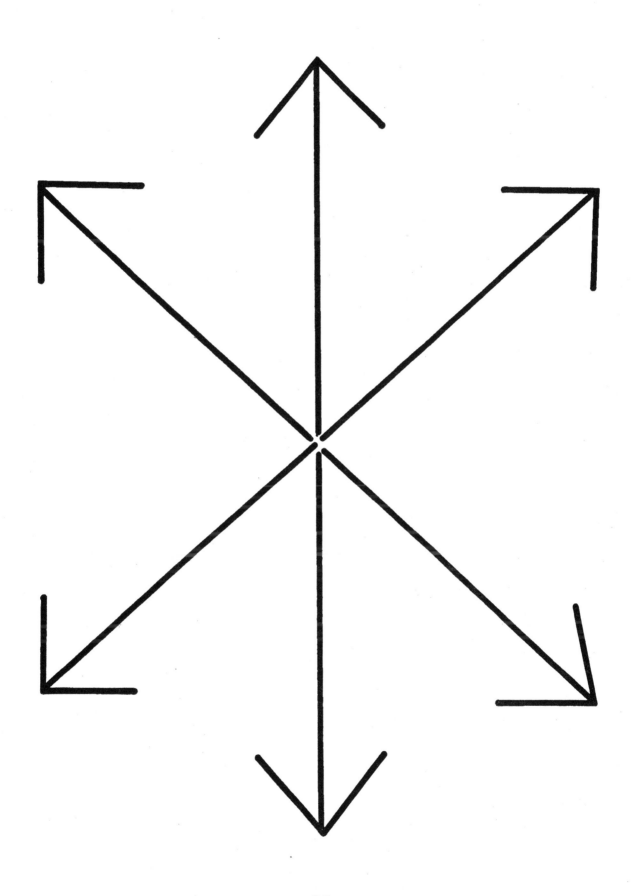

# Straw Snowflakes

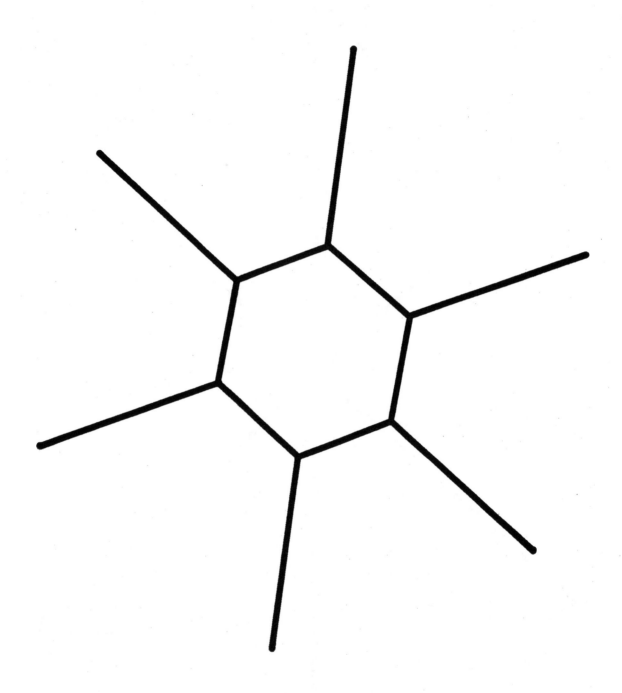

# Straw Snowflakes

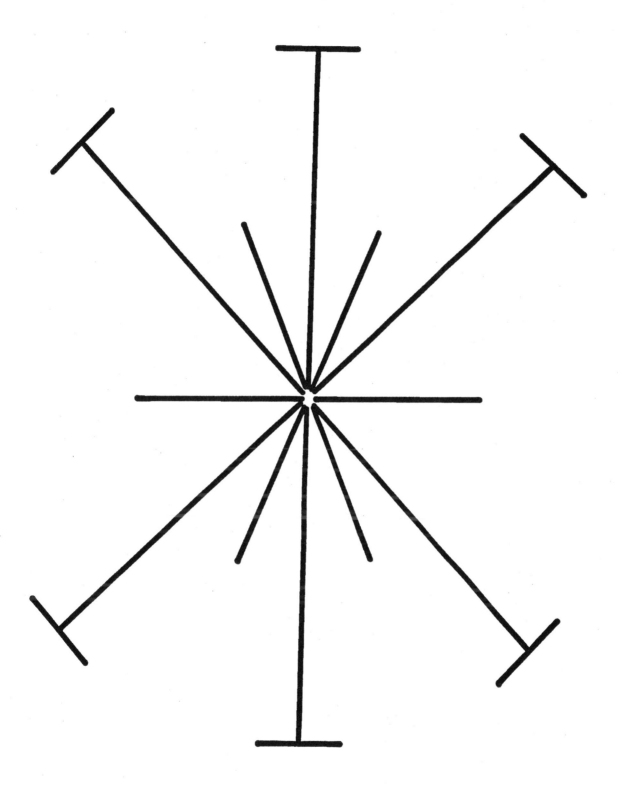

# Menorah Candles

**Themes**

Hanukkah

**Use With**

Individuals

Small Groups

**Skills**

Hand Strength

Finger and
Hand
Coordination

Count Objects

One-to-One
Correspondence

## Materials and Supplies

Clay

### Make Your MENORAH PAGES

1. Duplicate 4-6 copies of the MENORAH on the next page.
2. Laminate or cover each one with clear Contact® paper.

## Activity

When a child wants to put the candles in the menorah give her some clay and a MENORAH PAGE. First encourage her to soften her clay by squeezing and pounding it. Then divide it into 9 clumps, putting one clump on each circle beneath the menorah. Now have her roll each clump into a candle and place it on the menorah. All done? Count the candles.

# Menorah Candles

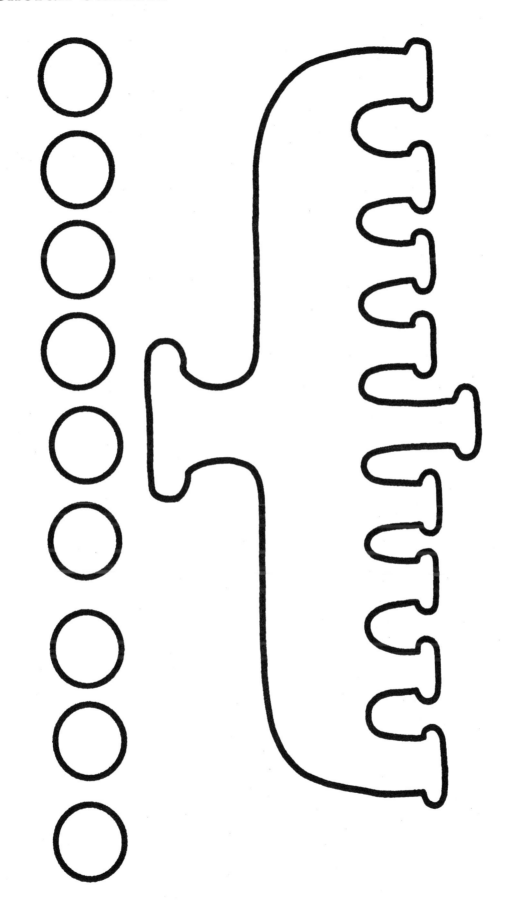

# Hanukkah Hide

## Themes

Hanukkah

Other Festivals, such as birthdays, which traditionally have candles

## Use With

Individuals

Small Groups

## Skills

Tactile Discrimination

One-to-One Correspondence

Count Objects

## Materials and Supplies

9 birthday candles for each menorah

Sand

1 plastic tub for each menorah

9 thread spools for each menorah

1, 12" strip of smooth wood, such as the backside of a wooden ruler, for each menorah

### Make Your SPOOL MENORAH

1. Glue 9 thread spools on a strip of wood.
2. Let dry.

## Activity

Fill the plastic tubs with sand. Hide 9 candles in each tub. Set the menorahs next to the tubs.

Have the children sift through the sand with their hands and find the candles. As they find each one, place it in the menorah. Count the candles with the children as they find them, and then count how many more they need. Continue until all the candles have been found and the menorah is complete. Take the candles out, hide them, and play HANUKKAH HIDE again – and again – and again. It's really fun!

### Play Again – It's Fun!

*Happy Birthday* – Glue the spools around the edge of a small pizza board. Hide the candles in the sand, as above. After the children have found all the candles, sing HAPPY BIRTHDAY. Great game to play on children's birthdays.

# Dreidel Painting

## Themes

Hanukkah

## Use With

Individuals

## Skills

Eye-Hand
  Coordination

Finger
  Coordination

## Materials and Supplies

Plastic dreidels

Different colors of poster paint

Small containers

Shoe box lids

Paper cut to fit inside the shoe box lids

## Activity

Pour one color of paint into each container. Set a dreidel in each one. Put the box lids, paper, and paint on the table.

Remind the children to put on smocks. Have each of them put a sheet of paper in their box lid and choose a dreidel from one container. Spin it like a top on their paper. Encourage them to continue DREIDEL PAINTING, using as many colors as they choose. HAPPY HANUKKAH!

# Decorated Trees

## Themes

Christmas

5 Senses

## Use With

Individuals

Small Groups

## Skills

Tactile Discrimination

Arm, Hand, and Finger Coordination

## Materials and Supplies

Stickers (stars, circles, etc.)

Tape

Green crayons with the paper removed

White paper

### Make and Decorate Your CHRISTMAS TREES

1. Cut out 5-6 construction paper Christmas trees. (See pattern on the next page.)

2. Decorate each tree by randomly putting stickers on it. Use long pieces of tape for garland.

## Activity

Make loops of tape. Put several on the back of each tree. Stick the trees to the top of a table. (Leave space between them so children have room to stand and work.) Put the crayons in a tub and set near the trees.

Have the children put white paper over the Christmas trees. Show them how to rub their crayons over the trees so they appear on the white paper. When finished, the children may want to cut out their trees and decorate them with stickers and/or crayons.

### Play Again – It's Fun!

*More Tree Rubbings*: Instead of sticking the trees to a table top, stick them to clipboards with white paper on top. Let children take the clipboards to favorite spots in the room and make their rubbings.

**Decorated Trees**

# Soft Dough Ornaments

## Themes

Christmas

## Use With

Individuals

Small Groups

## Skills

Finger
  Coordination

Eye-Hand
  Coordination

Parts/Whole

Play Together

## Materials and Supplies

Several different colors of
  soft dough/modeling
  clay

4-5 pieces of green
  posterboard

### Make Your CHRISTMAS TREES

1. Using the tree shape as
   a model, draw a
   Christmas tree on each
   piece of green posterboard.

2. Laminate or cover each Christmas tree with clear
   Contact®paper.

## Activity

Put several Christmas trees and
dough/clay on the table. Let the
children pinch off small pieces of
dough/clay, roll them into balls, and
put them on the tree. Continue
adding as many "ornaments" as the
children would like. After the tree is
full of "ornaments," let the children
press and flatten them with their
index fingers.

*Berry Trees*: Cut evergreen trees as
above. Let the children use green
dough to make little berries. Stick
them all over the tree.

# Soft Dough Ornaments

# Candy Canes

## Themes

Christmas

## Use With

Individuals

Small Groups

## Skills

Visual Motor Control

Eye-Hand Coordination

## Materials and Supplies

Green and red bingo markers

Heavy paper or tagboard

### Make Your CANDY CANES

1. Cut out paper/tagboard candy cane shapes.

2. Draw diagonal stripes on each CANE.

## Activity

Set the CANES and markers on the table. Have the children dot along each stripe. Encourage them to make each dot touch the previous one.

### Hint

- If you have older children, let them use CANDY CANE stencils to make their own CANES, cut them out and add the diagonal stripes. Now the children are ready to dot their CANES.

### Play Again – It's Fun!

*Barber Poles*: You'll need paper towel rolls, red and white paint in shallow containers, and sponge applicators from shoe polish bottles. Let the children paint alternate stripes on their POLES.

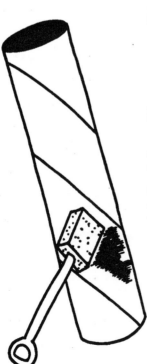

**Candy Canes**

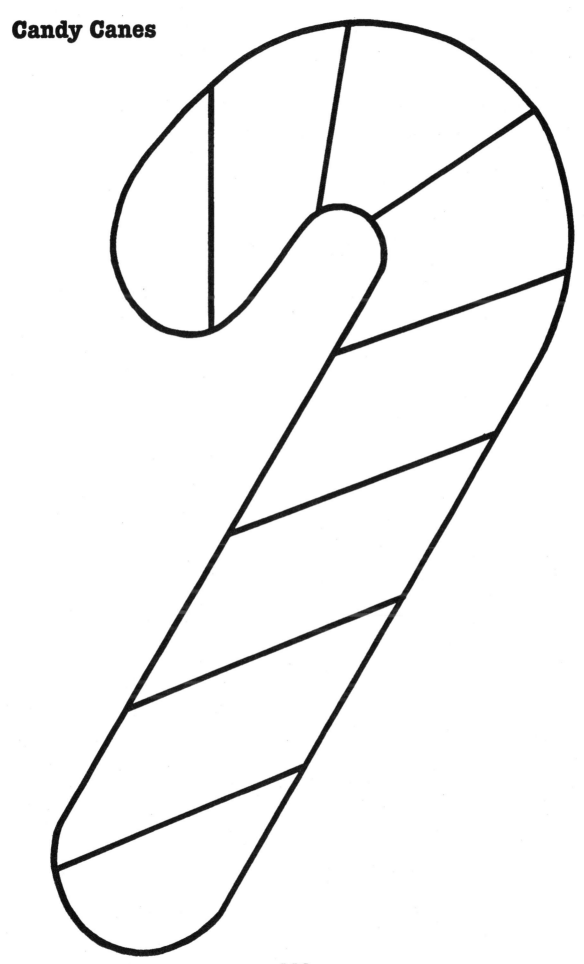

# Holiday Wreath

## Themes

Christmas

## Use With

Individuals

Small Groups

## Skills

Hand Strength

Eye-Hand
  Coordination

Cooperation

Play Together

## Materials and Supplies

Green posterboard

Small self-adhesive red dots

## Activity

Using pinking shears, cut a large posterboard wreath shape. Set it on the table with lots of small red sticker dots. Let the children stick "berries" to their wreath. Add a bow and hang on the classroom door at the children's eye level.

### Play Again – It's Fun

*Holiday Wreaths For Home*: Cut lots of 7" green and red construction paper circles with the centers cut out. Encourage the children to randomly punch lots of holes around their green wreaths. Turn the wreaths over and have the children brush the backsides with watered-down glue. Stick the red circle on the glue and gently rub it. Turn it over and see all the holly berries.

Add a bow it you'd like. Take home for a holiday decoration.

# Greeting Card Rubbings

## Themes

Holidays

## Use With

Individuals

Small Groups

## Skills

Hand Strength

Visual Motor
   Control

## Materials and Supplies

Holiday cards with raised designs

Crayons with the paper removed

Clipboards

## Activity

Have each child choose a card and cover it with
white paper. Clip the card and paper on a clipboard.
Have the children hold their crayons flat against the
paper and rub until the entire design is visible.

# Kwanzaa Gifts

## Themes

Kwanzaa

## Use With

Small Groups

Large Groups

## Skills

Hand Strength

Eye-Hand
Coordination

Visual
Discrimination

## Materials and Supplies

Pieces of aluminum foil, cut in a variety of sizes

Large box

## Activity

Set the box in the middle of the room.

During free choice have the children choose pieces of
foil and find objects in the room small enough to be
wrapped in each one. Wrap the objects and put them
in the box. Encourage the children to find and wrap
as many objects as they'd like.

Bring the gift box to circle time. Have a child choose
a gift, guess what it could be, and then unwrap it.
Hold it up and everyone call out what it is.

# Kwanzaa Harvest

## Themes

Kwanzaa

Other Harvest
  Festivals
  such as
  Thanksgiving

Farm

Foods/
  Nutrition

## Use With

Small Groups

## Skills

Motor Planning

Body
  Coordination

Play Together

Cooperation

## Materials and Supplies

Scooter boards

Plastic fruits and vegetables

Empty box or basket

## Activity

In a large open area, scatter plastic fruits and vegetables on the floor. Set the basket in the middle.

Have the children ride their scooter boards, "harvesting" the fruits and vegetables. Encourage them to pick up the produce one at a time and put it in the basket. Continue until all the fruits and vegetables have been "harvested."

# Bear's Path

## Themes

Winter

Forest Animals

Bears

## Use With

Individuals

Small Groups

## Skills

Motor Planning

Body
 Coordination

## Materials and Supplies

Large box – Big enough for several children to sit in

Bear paws

20'-30' length of paper (plastic carpet runner used in
 some church weddings or an old window shade)

### Make Your BEAR CAVE AND PATH

1. Cut the top off the box. Let the children paint the
 box gray. This will be the BEAR CAVE.

2. Cut out about 20-26, 6" black construction paper
 circles for bear paws. Glue the paws on the paper
 in pairs, approximately 12" apart. Use markers to
 add nails to the claws.

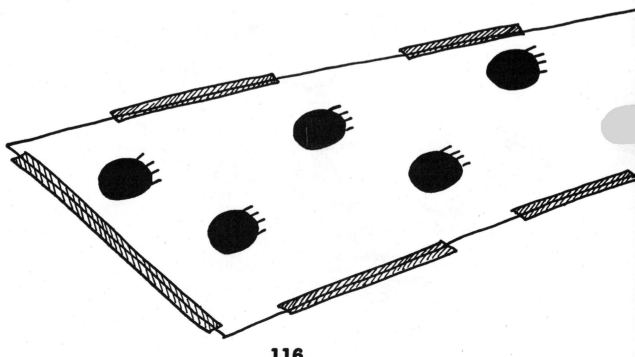

# Activity

Securely tape the BEAR PATH to the floor and put the CAVE at the end.

Have the children "walk" the BEAR PATH by putting each hand and foot on a paw. Encourage them to move forward by first moving their hands and then their feet to the next pairs of paws. When the children reach the CAVE, encourage them to go inside and rest.

**Hint:**

- Put 5-6 books about bears in the bear cave. While the children are resting, they can read BROWN BEAR, BROWN BEAR WHAT DO YOU SEE? by Bill Martin, TIME TO SLEEP by Denise Fleming, and others.

# Bear's Journey

## Themes

Winter

Bears

Forest Animals

## Use With

Small Groups

Large Groups

## Skills

Motor Planning

Body
  Coordination

Play Together

## Materials and Supplies

Large box with one end cut open for the BEAR CAVE

Tunnel, large boxes

Blanket, sheet, chairs

Cushions, pillows, foam wedges

### Make Your PATH FOR THE BEAR'S JOURNEY

1.  In a large open area set up the bear's journey in the following order, using one item for each step:

    **Through** – Begin the journey with a tunnel or large cut out box for the "bears" to crawl through.

    **Under** – Loosely tape two sides of a blanket or sheet to the floor. Be sure it is loose enough to easily crawl under. Set a table or chair along the PATH.

    **In** – Box.

    **Over** – Set a cushion, pillow, or wedge on the floor for the "bears" to crawl over.

2.  Repeat the sequence making the journey as long as space allows.

## Activity

Have the children pretend to be "bears" and walk along the BEAR PATH. At the end of the JOURNEY, let them crawl into the CAVE and watch the other "bears." When the CAVE is full, have the "bears" crawl out and one at a time, repeat the JOURNEY in reverse.

### Hint:

*   Let the children wear bear headbands while on their JOURNEY.

**118**

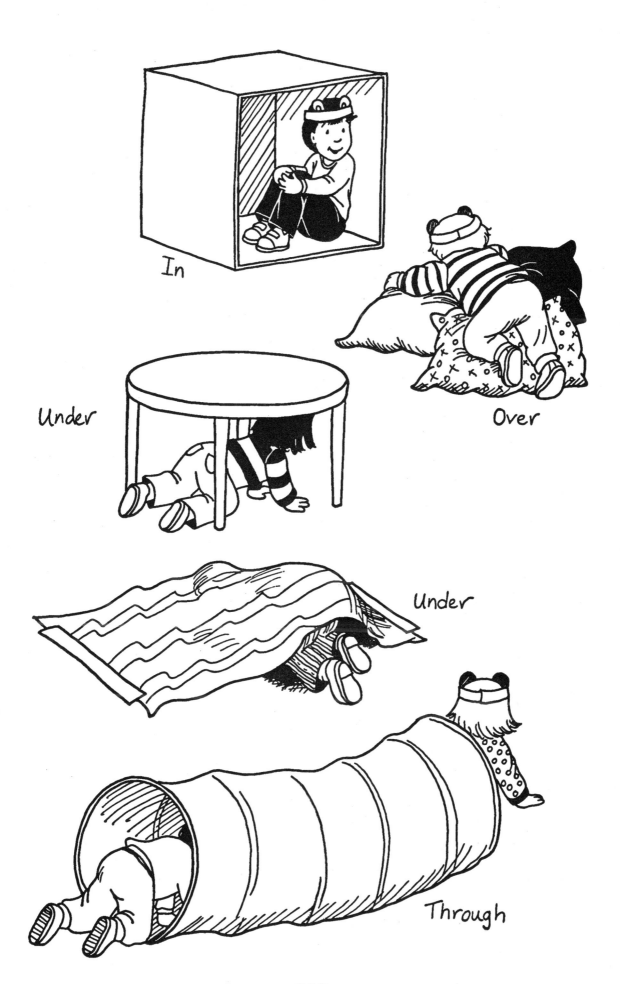

In

Over

Under

Under

Through

119

# Martin Luther King, Jr. Puzzle

## Themes

Martin Luther King, Jr. Birthday

## Use With

Individuals

Small Groups

## Skills

Visual Motor Control

Eye-Hand Coordination

Parts/Whole

## Materials and Supplies

Scissors

Pencils

Crayons including skin tone colors

Several 9"x12" produce trays

Sandwich bags

### Make Your MARTIN LUTHER KING, JR. PAGES

1. Duplicate the face of MARTIN LUTHER KING, JR. on the next page – at least one for each child.

2. Back each one on a piece of construction paper.

## Activity

Have the supplies on the table. Let each child color his puzzle if he wants, and then make the puzzle design by drawing several lines/curves from edge to edge. While he's making his lines, talk about how he will cut along them, making 2 or 4 or 6 pieces in his puzzle. Let the children cut out their puzzles. As they cut, put their pieces on produce trays. (Help if necessary.) Encourage the children to put their puzzles together.

After playing for as long as each would like, put each child's pieces in a sandwich bag, write his name on the bag, and let the children take them home. Encourage everyone to enjoy the puzzles with their families.

# Martin Luther King Jr. Puzzle

# Groundhog Scramble

## Themes

Groundhog Day

Forest Animals

Animal Homes

## Use With

Individuals

Small Groups

## Skills

Visual Control

Eye-Hand Coordination

## Materials and Supplies

3-4 small containers

Large marbles (Groundhogs)

4-5 toilet paper tubes

## Activity

In an open, carpeted area, tape toilet paper tubes to the floor at various angles approximately 6" from the wall. Put a long straight taped line about 3' from the tubes. Place 10-15 large marbles in each container.

Have the children lie on their tummies behind the taped line. Give each child a container of marbles (groundhogs). Have the children help the "groundhogs" scramble back to their "holes" by carefully rolling the marbles towards the tubes.

**Play Again – It's Fun!**

*More Groundhog Scramble* – Another time use ping-pong balls or tennis balls with paper cups. A great variation for younger children.

# Bows and Boxes

## Materials and Supplies

Scooter boards

Lots of sticky bows

Large box covered with wrapping paper

## Activity

Set the box in the middle of a large open area. Scatter the bows on the floor away from the box.

Have the children lie on the scooter boards, scoot to the bows, and then scoot over to the box and stick their bows on it. Continue until all the bows are picked up and sticking on the box.

### Play Again – It's Fun!

*Add a "Red" Bow:* As each child gets on his scooter board, tell him which color bow to pick up and stick on the box. *"Jose, scoot over to a 'red' bow, pick it up and then go stick it on the box."*

*Sit On the Scooters:* Have the children sit on their scooters and pull with their hands and/or feet.

*Give a Gift:* Wrap the lid and bottom separately. After the box is decorated, fill it with paper products for the local shelter, etc.

# Letter Carrier Routes

## Themes

Occupations
Valentine's Day

## Use With

Small Groups
Large Groups

## Skills

Motor Planning
Body
  Coordination
Reading
  Pictures

## Materials and Supplies

3-4 different colors of masking tape

Shoe boxes for "mailboxes"

Construction paper

3-4 small tote bags for "mail bags"

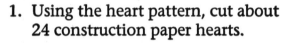

### Make Your VALENTINE ACTION CARDS

1. Using the heart pattern, cut about 24 construction paper hearts.

2. Duplicate 3 of each ACTION PICTURE on pages 126-129.

3. Cut out the ACTION PICTURES and glue each one to the middle of a heart. Now you have 3 sets of VALENTINE ACTION CARDS. Put a CARD in each "mail bag."

4. **Optional:** Laminate or cover each VALENTINE ACTION CARD with clear Contact® paper.

## Activity

In a large open area tape 3 or 4 mail "routes" to the floor (straight, curvy, zig-zag, looping). Set a "mailbox" at the end of each route. Set one "mailbag" at the beginning of each "route."

Have the children take turns delivering the VALENTINE ACTION CARDS by looking at the ACTION CARD in their bags and jumping, skipping, crawling, etc. down the "route." When he gets to the "mailbox" he should deliver the CARD. Return to the beginning, get another CARD, and play again.

## Play Again – It's Fun!

*Faster Delivery*: Have the children ride tricycles, big wheels, hoppity hops, and/or scooter boards to deliver the VALENTINE ACTION CARDS.

*Deliver Junk Mail:* Instead of gluing the action pictures on hearts, glue them on old junk mail. Play as above.

# Letter Carrier's Route ACTION CARDS

# Punch and Sew Hearts

## Themes

Hearts
Valentine's Day

## Use With

Individuals
Small Groups

## Skills

Hand Strength
Eye-Hand
 Coordination
Creativity

## Materials and Supplies

Pink, red, white construction paper – other colors if
 your children want

Yarn

3-4 blunt-tipped needles or masking tape

3-4 hand-held hole punches

### Make Your HEARTS

1. Using the heart shape on the next page, cut out
 lots of different colored hearts for your children.

2. Using a wide marker, make dots about 1" apart,
 around the edge of each heart.

3. Thread each needle with yarn or tape one end of
 the yarn with a little masking tape to form a
 point.

## Activity

Give each child a
HEART and a hole
punch. Have him
punch a hole on each
dot. Tape the loose end
of the yarn at the
starting point.
Encourage the
children to sew all
around their hearts.

After sewing, let the
children decorate their
HEARTS with stamps,
stickers, bingo
markers, collage
materials, etc.

130

# Punch and Sew Hearts

# Fill Up the Heart

## Themes

Hearts

Valentine's Day

## Use With

Individuals

Small Groups

## Skills

Arm, Hand, and Finger Coordination

Eye-Hand Coordination

Creativity

## Materials and Supplies

Red, pink, and white construction paper – other colors your children choose

Glue

Several small containers such as margarine tubs

### Make Your HEARTS and STRIPS

1. Cut out lots of large colored hearts for your children.

2. Cut lots of 1"x11" red, pink, and white construction paper strips. Put the different colored strips on paper plates or trays.

## Activity

Set the supplies on the table. Let each child tear several strips into short pieces and put them in a small container. Next encourage them to choose a heart and glue the pieces inside the heart. Continue gluing until their hearts are full of color. (Tear more strips as needed.)

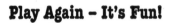

### Play Again – It's Fun!

*More HEARTS*: Have a bucket of colored bingo markers plus all the other supplies. Repeat the activity above. After the children have finished gluing the strips, let them fill-in the spaces on their hearts with bingo markers.

# Floor Heart Puzzle

## Themes

Hearts
Valentines

## Use With

Individuals
Small Groups

## Skills

Visual Control
Eye-Hand
  Coordination
Cooperation

## Materials and Supplies

Large piece of pink posterboard

Several purple, blue, and red bingo markers

### Make Your HEART SHAPES

1. Draw the outline of a huge heart on the posterboard.
2. Write "I ♥ U" in large letters in the middle of the heart.

## Activity

Set the supplies on the table. When children want to work on the giant puzzle, show them how to use the purple bingo markers to dot along the outline of their heart. Encourage the children to make each dot touch the previous one. After covering the outline with dots, have the children use the bingo markers to dot the symbols in the middle.

After the HEART is dry, you and the children draw some lines and curves from edge to edge. Then cut on the lines to make the FLOOR PUZZLE.

Lay the pieces on the floor and let the children put it together.

### Play Again – It's Fun

*More Puzzles*: Use different shapes which relate to other themes and topics you are talking about with the children. For example, a leaf for fall, boat, airplane and/or car for transportation, child in bathing suit for summer, etc.

# Cherry Pie Relay

## Materials and Supplies

Spoon

Red pom-poms

Pie pans

## Activity

Divide the children into teams with half of each team at opposite ends of the gym. Team members stand in line. Give the first child for each team at one end of the gym a pom-pom and a spoon. Give the first child for each team at the other end of the gym one pie pan.

When you say *"Go!"* have the children holding "cherries" put them on their spoons and start walking to the middle of the gym. The children holding pie pans start walking to the middle of the gym. When they meet, each child with the "cherry" puts it in his team member's pie pan.

Both children return to their teams. The child with the spoon gives it to the next child who adds his "cherry" and the other child passes the pie pan to the next player. Continue until all the teams have finished their CHERRY PIES.

134

# Pass Lincoln's Hat

## Materials and Supplies

Plastic hat or Abe Lincoln style headband

Record player or tape recorder

## Activity

Have the children stand in a circle. Give the hat to one of the children. Start the music and have the children begin passing the hat. Stop the music. The child holding the hat turns and faces outside the circle, but continues to play. Start the music again and pass the hat. Each time the music stops, the child holding the hat changes to face outside or returns to face inside the circle.

**Play Again – It's Fun!**

*Pass the Firefighter Helmet*: Instead of using the plastic hat or Abe Lincoln style hat, use a firefighter helmet. Great activity for October–Fire Safety Month.

*Another Hat*: Use any other type of hat to accent the theme, season, or holiday you are focusing on. For example use a rain hat on a rainy spring day.

# Shamrock Fill-In

**Themes**

St. Patrick's Day

**Use With**

Individuals

Small Groups

**Skills**

Visual Motor Control

Finger Strength

## Materials and Supplies

Green fingerpaint

Shamrock shapes

## Activity

Make 20 or more copies of the shamrock shape on the next page. Pour the fingerpaint into shallow trays. Place the shamrocks and fingerpaint on the table.

Have the children dip and re-dip their fingers in paint and make fingerprints all around the inside edge of the shamrocks. Some children may want to make second and third outlines around the inside of their shamrocks. Still others may want to fill the entire inside of their shamrocks.

### Play Again – It's Fun!

*More Green Shamrocks*: Have each child put a spoonful of green fingerpaint in the middle of her shamrock. Encourage her to use all her fingers to spread it around. Continue until the shamrock is full of green paint.

*With Bingo Markers*: Use green bingo markers instead of fingerprints to make dots around the inside edges of the shamrocks.

# Shamrock Fill-In

# Spring Hunt

## Themes

Spring

## Use With

Small Groups

Large Groups

## Skills

Motor Planning

Body
  Coordination

Recognizing
  Colors

## Materials and Supplies

Large blanket

Large plastic eggs which
  "crack" into 2 pieces

Tiny "things" related to Spring, such as:

  Rubber worms

  Baby animals

  Flowers

  Birds

  Butterflies

## Activity

Put the little Spring things inside the eggs. Lay the eggs on the floor. Cover them with the blanket.

Have the children sit around the blanket and hold the edges. Name a child and tell her what color egg to get. She crawls under the blanket, finds that color egg, and crawls back out. Continue until all the eggs have been found. Let the children open their eggs and see what's inside. Have everyone tell the others what he found in his egg. Close the eggs back up.

### Hint:

* Have the children, who are holding the blanket, hold it a little higher while the child is crawling under it. When the child is back out, lay the blanket down again.

### Play Again – It's Fun!

*Find the Eggs:* Have a large bucket in the sand table. Hide the colored eggs deep in the sand. Let the children use their hands to dig for them. As they find each one, open it up and see what's inside. Close it and put in the bucket. After all the eggs have been found, hide them and play again.

# Feather Pass

## Themes

Birds

Spring

Wind and Air

## Use With

Small Groups

Large Groups

## Skills

Visual Motor
Control

Eye-Hand
Coordination

Control of
Facial Muscles

Play Together

## Materials and Supplies

Small fluffy feather/s

## Activity

Have the children sit in a circle with their open
hands together and their palms turned up.

Set a feather in one child's hands. Have him gently
blow it to a child sitting next to him. That child
catches it in her open hands. She turns and blows it
to the next child. Continue passing the feather
around the circle until everyone has had several
turns.

**Hint:**

- If you are playing with a large group of children,
  start several feathers at different points in the
  circle.

# Animals Go Home

## Themes

Animal Homes

Animals

Spring

## Use With

Individuals

Small Groups

## Skills

Visual Control

Eye-Hand
  Coordination

## Materials and Supplies

Lots of 3"x15" strips of paper (adding machine tape)

Different colored bingo markers

### Make Your ANIMAL PATHS

1. Duplicate the animals and their homes on pages 143-145.

2. Color them if you want.

3. Glue the animals on the left ends of the strips.

4. Glue the matching animal homes on the right ends of the strips.

5. Draw different PATHS on each strip leading from the animal to his home. (curved, zig-zag, straight, looping, etc.)

## Activity

Tape several ANIMAL PATHS to the edge of a table. Have the bingo markers in a bucket. Let the children use the bingo markers to "dot" each animal's way home.

When the first animals have followed the path home, take them off the table and hang them on the door at the children's eye level. Tape several more PATHS on the table and let the children help these animals find their way home.

# Animals Go Home

# Animals Go Home

# Animals Go Home

# Bunny's Memory

## Themes

Colors

Easter

## Use With

Individual

Small Groups

## Skills

Body
  Coordination

Motor Planning

Visual Memory

Matching

Color Names

## Materials and Supplies

Plastic bags with handles

Pairs of plastic eggs in a variety of colors – can even be more than one pair of the same color, such as 2 pairs of red eggs

Egg carton

## Activity

Put one set of the plastic eggs in a shallow container. Set it about 10-15 feet from where the children are sitting. Have the other set of plastic eggs behind your back.

Call on a child to hold the empty egg carton. Reach behind your back and get an egg. Set it in the first egg section. Encourage everyone to call out the color. Get another egg and call out its color. Continue with more eggs if you think the child holding the carton can remember more than two.

Have the child give you the egg carton. Give him a plastic bag. Have him hop to the container of eggs, pick out the eggs that match the ones in the carton and put them in his bag. Hop back.

When he returns, have the child hold up the eggs in his bag. One at a time put them in the egg carton next to the matching egg. If they all match, take them out and set them next to you. If not ask the child if he'd like to hop back and get the matching egg. Continue playing BUNNY MEMORY with different children pretending to be the bunny.

### Hint:

- You might want several children to be bunnies at one time.

# Collect the Eggs

## Themes

Easter

## Use With

Individuals

Small Groups

## Skills

Body
    Coordination

Motor Planning

Taking Turns

## Materials and Supplies

Hula hoops

Baskets with handles

Colored construction/wallpaper paper eggs

## Activity

Set up the trail by placing the hoops on the floor in a curving line. Have each hoop touch the hoop in front of and behind it. Place the eggs along the trail outside each hoop.

Give a child a basket. Starting at one end of the trail, have him hop from hoop to hoop picking up one egg at each hoop. Let the children take turns until all the eggs are picked up. Let several children put the eggs back along the trail and play again.

### Hint:

- If hula hoops aren't available, mark the trail with masking tape.

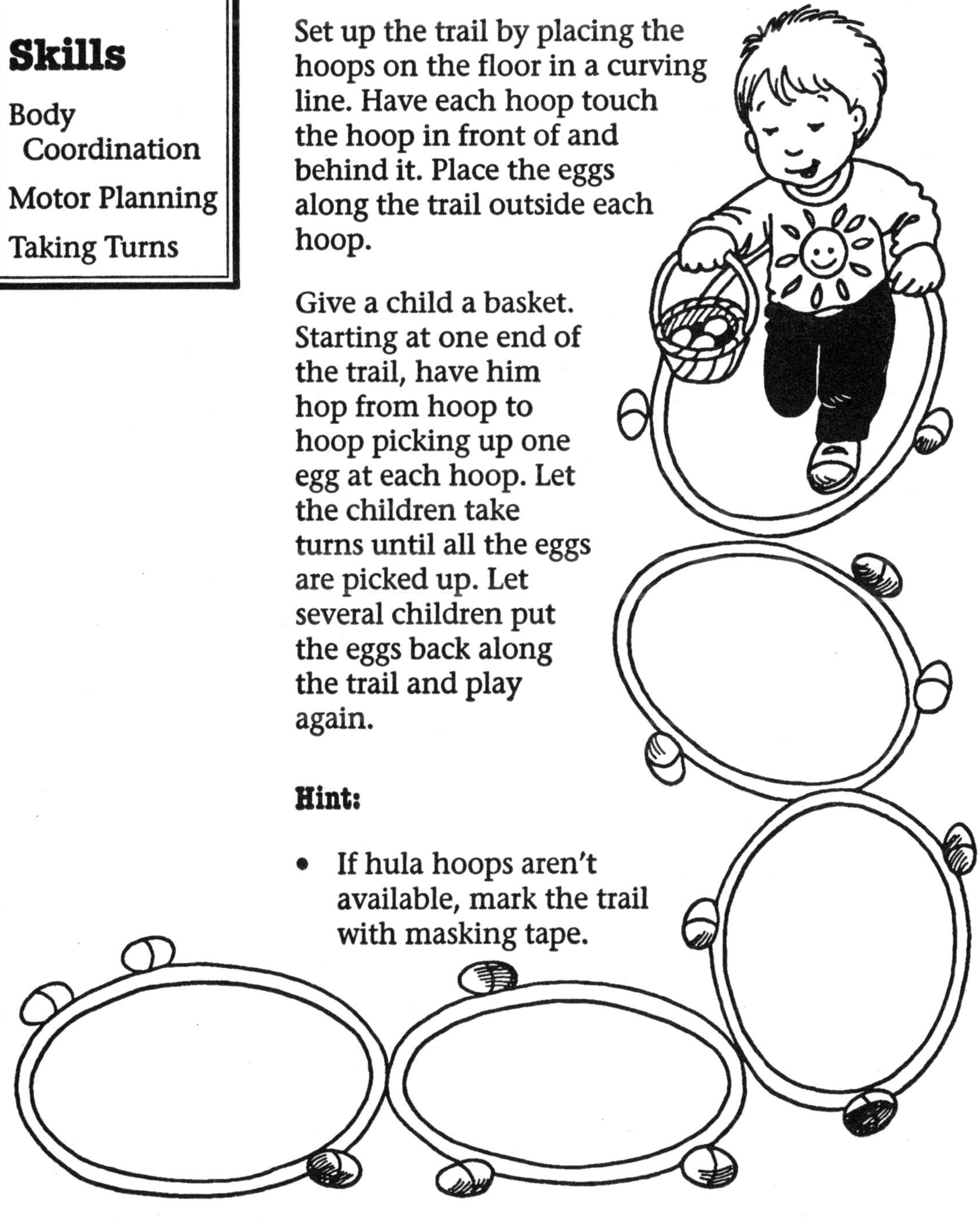

147

# Hopping Down the Bunny Trail

## Themes

Easter

Spring

Animals

## Use With

Small Groups

Large Groups

## Skills

Motor Planning

Body
  Coordination

**Make Your BUNNY TRAIL**

1. Using the bunny feet mini pattern as a guide, make a large template.

2. Cut a long sheet of butcher paper or use a long solid color window shade.

3. Use the large template to create the BUNNY TRAIL. Make a series of "hops" down the length of the paper/shade. Make some of the "hops" close together, some farther apart, others sideways and even more off to one side or the other.

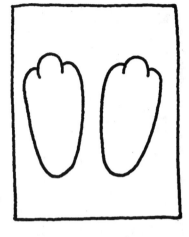

## Materials and Supplies

Bunny trail

Tape

## Activity

In an open area tape the BUNNY TRAIL to the floor. Encourage the children to HOP DOWN THE BUNNY TRAIL, trying to keep their feet close together.

### Hints

- If children are just learning to hop, you can help them by chanting, *"hop, hop, hop..."* as they move down the TRAIL.

- Other "bunnies" might like you to hold their hands while they hop. After several times, encourage them to try it by themselves. You'll watch!

### Play Again – It's Fun!

*Collect the Eggs:* Place lots of plastic or paper eggs along the BUNNY TRAIL. Have each child carry a basket and collect eggs as she hops down the trail.

# Stuffed Bunnies

**Themes**

Easter

Spring Animals

**Use With**

Individuals

Small Groups

**Skills**

Hand Strength

Eye-Hand
Coordination

Cooperation

## Materials and Supplies

White plastic bags

Newspaper

2, 14" pieces of heavy yarn

### Draw Your BUNNY FACES

1. Have several medium size white plastic bags. Using permanent colored markers, draw a large bunny face on each bag.

1.

2.

3.

## Activity

Have the children help you tear the sheets of newspaper into 4 pieces. Put the pieces near the bunny bags.

Have the children crumple each piece of newspaper into a small tight ball and toss it into a bunny bag. After each bag is stuffed about 2/3 full, roll the edge down, form ears with the 2 ends and tie them.

Use the STUFFED BUNNIES in learning centers and/or just outside the classroom door to "welcome" everyone each day.

# Jelly Bean Jar

## Themes

Easter

Colors

Foods

Five Senses

## Use With

Individuals

Small Groups

## Skills

Tactile
  Discrimination

Eye-Hand
  Coordination

Color Names

Play Together

## Materials and Supplies

Crayons with the paper removed

Butcher/newsprint paper to fit the art table

Tape

Lots of different size jelly bean shapes cut out of
  tagboard, corrugated cardboard, and/or textured
  wallpaper

## Activity

Cut the butcher paper into a
huge jar shape.

Have the children help you
spread the different size jelly
beans all around the table.
(Tape them down if you want.) Lay the jelly bean jar
over the jelly beans. Tape the corners to the table so
the paper does not slide around. Set the crayons on
the table.

Let each child feel around the top of the paper until
he finds a jelly bean. When he locates one, have him
choose a crayon and rub over it until the shape
appears. Encourage the children to continue feeling,
finding, and
coloring the
jelly beans
different colors
until the jar is
filled with
colorful jelly
beans. Hang it
up for everyone
to see. (Talk
about all the
different
colors.)

151

# Pass the Eggs

**Themes**

Animals

Spring

Easter

**Use With**

Small

Large Groups

**Skills**

Motor Planning

Eye-Hand
  Coordination

Pass Objects

Play Together

## Materials and Supplies

Several inflatable/plastic eggs

## Activity

Have the children stand in a circle. Give 2 or 3 children an egg. Begin to slowly chant, *"Pass, pass, pass the eggs."* As you chant, have the children twist at their waists and pass the eggs around the circle at the speed you are chanting. When you stop chanting, the children stop passing. (The children may want to chant with you as they pass the eggs.)

Chant at a different speed and encourage the children to pass the eggs at the new speed. Continue chanting and playing at different speeds. (You could reverse and pass the eggs in the opposite direction.)

**Play Again – It's Fun!**

*More Pass the Eggs*: Next time you play have the children kneel or sit.

*Pass More Things:* Instead of passing an egg, pick an object that highlights the theme you are focusing on. For example:

- Soft bunny for spring.
- Beach ball for summer.
- Football for fall.
- Pumpkin for harvest.
- Snowpal for winter fun.

# Fill Up the Carton

## Themes

Food

Farm

Easter

## Use With

Small Groups

## Skills

Upper Body Control

Cooperation

One-to-One Correspondence

## Materials and Supplies

Plastic eggs

Egg carton

Egg basket

## Activity

Have the children work in groups of three:

1. One child lies on the floor with his knees bent and feet flat on the floor.

2. Another child sits at the first child's feet, holding the empty egg carton.

3. The third child sits near the first child's head, holding the basket of eggs.

The child lying down reaches his arms over his head, grabs an egg, sits up and puts it in the egg carton. He repeats this until he has FILLED UP THE CARTON. The children change places and play again.

# Polka Dot Eggs

## Themes

Colors

Easter

## Use With

Individuals

Small Groups

## Skills

Eye-Hand
Coordination

Visual Motor
Control

Color Patterns

## Materials and Supplies

Different colored bingo markers

### Make Your EGG SHAPES

1. Cut out lots of large construction paper EGG
   SHAPES.

2. Draw different lines across each one. (See
   illustration.)

## Activity

Put the markers in the middle of the table. When
children want to do the activity, first let them pick out
egg shapes. Using any colors they choose, have them
carefully dot along the lines on their eggs. Encourage
them to make each dot touch the previous one.

**Hint:**

- Encourage
  older children
  to make color
  patterns such
  as pink-green,
  pink-green,
  pink-green, etc.

# Polka Dot Eggs

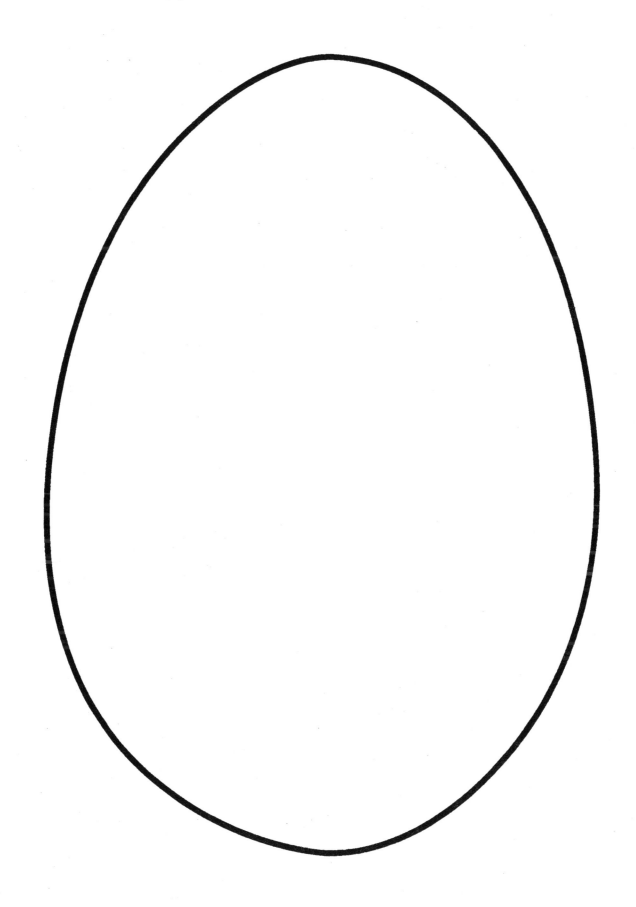

# Egg Hunt

## Themes

Spring

Easter

## Use With

Individuals

Small Groups

## Skills

Body
 Coordination

Play Together

## Materials and Supplies

Lots of 5 ounce paper cups

Small plastic eggs

Scooter boards

Basket or nest

## Activity

Place the cups all around the floor of a large open area. Put eggs under all/most of the cups. Set the basket/nest off to the side.

Have the children stand together. Say, *"Egg hunt."* The children each hop to one of the paper cups, lift it up, put the egg in the cup, and hop over to the basket. Dump the egg in the basket. Set the cup in a stack next to it. Hop to another egg and continue playing. Keep encouraging the children to hop around the whole area until all the eggs have been found and put in the basket.

### Play Again – It's Fun!

*More Hunting*: Hide other objects under the cups to coordinate with the theme, season, or holiday you are focusing on. For example:

- Worms for Spring – wiggle around the area

- Snowflakes for Winter or Weather – dance around the area

- Bingo Chips for Color – crawl around the area

- Shells for the Beach or Summer – float around the area

# Egg Pick-Up

## Themes

Spring

Easter

## Use With

Individuals

Small Groups

## Skills

Finger
Coordination

Visual Motor
Control

One-to-One
Correspondence

## Materials and Supplies

24 plastic or styrofoam eggs

Several very small paper cups

2 empty egg cartons

Large plastic tub

## Activity

Set a large plastic tub on a table. Fill it about half full
of water. Put the eggs in the water. Have the paper
cups and egg carton/s on the table.

Let several children stand around the tub and use the
cups to scoop the eggs out of the water, one at a
time, and put them in an egg carton. Encourage the
children to continue until the egg cartons are full.
Dump the eggs back in the water and fill the cartons
again.

**Hint:**

- Poke a hole in the bottom of each cup to let the
  water drain out.

**Play Again –
It's Fun!**

*Scoop the Eggs:*
Put several
large slotted
spoons on the
table. Have the
children use
the spoons to
SCOOP THE
EGGS and set
them in the egg
carton.

# Earth Day Clean-Up

## Materials and Supplies

Plastic grocery bags with handles

Clean garbage can

Masking tape

"Litter" such as:

> Empty soda cans
> Candy wrappings
> Fast food containers
> Juice boxes and cans

"Work" gloves

## Activity

In an open area make several curved and winding masking tape paths approximately 20' long. Scatter the "litter" along the paths.

When a child wants to play, have him put on a pair of work gloves and give him a plastic bag. Have him walk along the path. Encourage him to stoop and pick up the "litter" along the way. At the end of the path, have him empty his bag into the garbage can.

**Play Again – It's Fun!**

*More Clean-Up –*

- Have the children jump, skip, hop, or crawl along the path.

- Make your winding paths with clothesline instead of masking tape.

- Simply scatter the "litter" in a large, open space. Let the children pick it up as they walk around the "littered" area.

159

# Cinco de Mayo Fireworks

## Themes

Cinco de Mayo

Other Festivals, such as the Fourth of July, which traditionally have fireworks

## Use With

Individuals

## Skills

Finger Coordination

Eye-Hand Coordination

Play Together

## Materials and Supplies

Green, white and red poster paint

3 large, flat containers such as brownie pans

Large sheets of dark blue or black paper or one long sheet of dark mural paper

3 or more medium or large size round balloons

## Activity

Fill the balloons (one for each container) with approximately one cup of water. Tie each closed. Pour shallow amounts of paint in each container. Set one balloon in each color of paint.

Give each child a piece of paper or tape the mural paper to the art table. Have the children put on smocks, hold the balloons by the knots and gently bounce them on the paper making splashes of red, green, and white "fireworks." Continue until the paper is full of brilliant, beautiful "fireworks."

### Play Again – It's Fun!

*Fourth of July Fireworks* – Use red, white, and light blue poster paint.

*Sock Fireworks* – Fill several knee socks with about one cup of sand. Knot the socks at the top. Set 1-2 socks next to each container of paint. Dip the socks in the paint and bounce them on the paper.

# Parachute Fireworks

## Themes

Cinco de Mayo

Other Festivals, such as Fourth of July, which traditionally have fireworks

Colors

## Use With

Small Groups

Large Groups

## Skills

Hand Strength

Body Coordination

Rote Counting

Cooperation

Play Together

## Materials and Supplies

$1/2$ sheets of red, white, and green construction paper

Parachute, large sheet, or blanket

## Activity

In a large open area, lay the parachute on the floor. Give each player several sheets of colored paper. Have them crumple the paper, one sheet at a time, in small, tight balls. Toss them on the parachute.

After all the balls are made, have the players hold the edge of the chute and stand up. Everyone count, *"uno, dos, tres, cuatro"* and on the count of *"cinco"* quickly raise and lower the parachute, launching the "fireworks" into the sky.

Collect the "fireworks" that flew off the parachute and play again and again.

# Eggs In the Nest

## Themes

Birds

Animal Homes

Spring

## Use With

Individuals

Small Groups

## Skills

Finger
Coordination

Hand Strength

Count Objects

Parts/Whole

## Materials and Supplies

Plastic place mats

Modeling clay or soft dough (Clay provides more
resistance for developing hand strength.)

## Activity

When a child wants to play, give her a place mat and
some clay/dough. Have her make a nest with half the
clay. Make the eggs by pinching off small pieces of
clay and rolling them into balls.

Put each "egg" in the nest. Continue adding as many
"eggs" as each child would like. *"How many eggs are
in your nest? Let's count."*

**Hints:**

- Count the "eggs"
  in the nests with
  the children.

- Find the largest
  and smallest
  "eggs" in the
  nests.

- Take the "eggs"
  out of the nest
  and form them
  into one large
  ball. Make more
  "eggs" for the
  nest.

- To make the
  activity a little
  easier, use
  artificial nests
  and have the
  children just
  make the eggs.

# Empty the Nest

## Themes

Birds

Animal Homes

Spring

## Use With

Individuals

Small Groups

## Skills

Hand Strength

Eye-Hand
  Coordination

Taking Turns

Counting
  Objects

## Materials and Supplies

Large brown grocery bag with the top rolled down low to make a "nest"

25-30 small plastic eggs

Tongs

Lunch bags

Regular or soft die (Make your own die by using permanent marker to put 1, 2, or 3 large dots on each side of a soft square block.)

## Activity

Put the "nest" on the table. Have the players sit around the "nest." Give each of them a lunch bag.

The first player rolls the die and counts the dots. (Let each child count her own dots or count them as a group.) Using the tongs, let the player remove that number of "eggs" from the "nest" and put them in her bag. Continue playing until the "nest" is empty.

# Shine the Light

## Themes

Spring

Baby Animals

Flowers

Any Theme or topic you are discussing with the children

## Use With

Individuals

Small Groups

## Skills

Visual Control

Eye-Hand Coordination

Give Directions

Follow Directions

## Materials and Supplies

Flashlight/s

Variety of spring pictures such as:

Baby animals

Flowers

Rain

Children wearing rain coats

Birds in nests

Worms on the sidewalk

Flowers!

## Activity

Lay the pictures on the table so the children can easily see all of them.

When a child wants to play, give him a flashlight. Name a picture, such as *"big pink flower," "yellow duckling,"* etc. The child SHINES THE LIGHT on the picture you named. Continue playing. After 4-5 pictures, switch places. Let the child name the pictures and you shine the light.

# Finger Cocoons

### Themes

Butterflies

Animal Homes

Spring

### Use With

Individuals

Small Groups

### Skills

Finger
  Coordination

Eye-Hand
  Coordination

## Materials and Supplies

Brown and/or green yarn

### Make Your COCOON LOOPS

1. Cut the yarn into one foot lengths.
2. Tie a LOOP at one end of each piece.

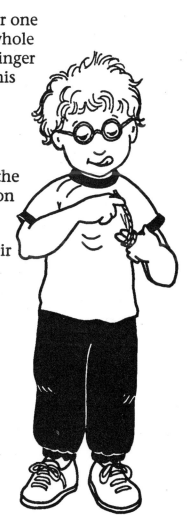

## Activity

When a child wants to make a FINGER COCOON, give him one piece of yarn. Have him slip the loop over one finger and then wrap the whole piece of yarn around that finger thus making a cocoon for his finger.

### Play Again – It's Fun!

*More Cocoons:* Encourage the children to make cocoons on different fingers. They can:

- Take one cocoon off their first finger and use the yarn to make another cocoon on a different finger.

- Use more pieces of yarn and make cocoons on as many fingers as each would like.

- Make "fat" cocoons by wrapping 2-3 fingers together.

# Blooming Colors

## Materials and Supplies

Small colored styrofoam plates

Food coloring/diluted poster paint

Plastic eye droppers

White construction paper

### Make Your FLOWERS and COLORS

1. Using the flower shapes on pages 167-169 cut out lots of different flowers from white construction paper.

2. Use food coloring and water to mix colored water with the children. Pour into small containers

## Activity

Have the supplies on the table. Let children drop colors of colored water/poster paint on their plates and then gently blow the colors around. Watch them flow together and mix. *"What new colors did you make?"* After each child has blown the colored water/ paint for as long as he wants, have him carefully lay a FLOWER CUT-OUT over the colors. Gently rub the back of the flower and then slowly pull it up. Let dry and hang for everyone to enjoy. Let the children repeat the activity as many times as each would like.

### Hint:

• Some children may want to add stems and leaves to their flowers.

### Play Again – It's Fun!

*More Blooming Colors:* Have children use straws to blow the colors around.

*Colorful Plates:* Using basters, drop colored water on paper plates and blow it around. Dry and hang.

# Blooming Colors

**Blooming Colors**

# Fly Beautiful Butterfly

## Themes

Butterflies

Animal Homes

Spring

## Use With

Pairs of
Children

## Skills

Eye-Hand
Coordination

Body Awareness

Imagination

Cooperation

## Materials and Supplies

Rolls of crepe paper

## Activity

Play FLY BEAUTIFUL BUTTERFLY in pairs. One child stands with his arms held snugly around the front of his waist. Have him hold onto one end of the roll of crepe paper. His partner wraps the crepe paper around the child's legs and upper body, thus spinning a cocoon for him.

When the cocoon is finished, the first child steps back and says, *"FLY BEAUTIFUL BUTTERFLY."* The second child pretends to be a butterfly as he "breaks out" and flies away as a newly emerged butterfly.

## WOW – HOW BEAUTIFUL AND GRACEFUL!

# Butterflies In the Wind

## Materials and Supplies

Plastic squeeze containers, such as those used for
  ketchup and mustard

Lots of tissue paper butterflies

## Activity

In a large open
area, give each
player a squeeze
bottle and a
butterfly. Have them
put their butterflies on
the floor and then
make them "fly" by
blowing them with
the squeeze bottles.

### Play Again –
It's Fun

*Along the Path:* Using colored
tape, make a long straight, zig-
zag, "S" curve, or "X" path.
Encourage the children to
blow their butterflies
ALONG THE PATH.

*More Objects In
the Wind:* Cut
out tissue
paper bats,
birds, fall
leaves,
snowflakes, etc.
and let the
children blow

# Tear and Stick Butterflies

## Themes

Butterflies

Spring
 Creatures

Color

Spring

## Use With

Individuals

Small Groups

## Skills

Finger
 Coordination

Eye-Hand
 Coordination

Cooperation

## Materials and Supplies

Several pieces of 11"x14" tagboard

Contact® paper

3" squares of construction paper, wrapping paper, and/or tissue paper

### Make Your BUTTERFLY TEMPLATES

1. Enlarge the BUTTERFLY on the next page.

2. Using the enlarged pattern, cut BUTTERFLY TEMPLATES in the pieces of tagboard.

3. Cut pieces of Contact® paper to cover the BUTTERFLY TEMPLATES.

## Activity

Put a BUTTERFLY, sticky side up on the table. Set the paper nearby.

Have the children tear very small pieces of paper and put them on the Contact® paper. Continue until the entire BUTTERFLY is full of color. Hang the BUTTERFLY from the ceiling. Put a second BUTTERFLY TEMPLATE on the table and let the children "color" another one.

# Tear and Stick Butterflies

# Colorful Kites

## Themes

Kites

Wind and Air

Spring

## Use With

Individuals

Small Groups

## Skills

Visual Motor Control

Eye-Hand Coordination

Create Stories

## Materials and Supplies

4-6 different size clear plastic lids

Colored pencils

White paper

### Make Your KITE TEMPLATES

1. Using the kite patterns on the next page, cut a different size KITE TEMPLATE into each plastic lid.

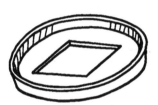

## Activity

Have the kite templates, paper, and colored pencils on the table. Let the children use the different templates to trace as many kites on their paper as each would like. Encourage them to use different sizes of kite templates and different colored pencils.

When each finishes, ask him if he'd like to color his kites and/or add tails to them. Maybe he'd like to dictate a sentence or even a story about his kites. Write what he says.

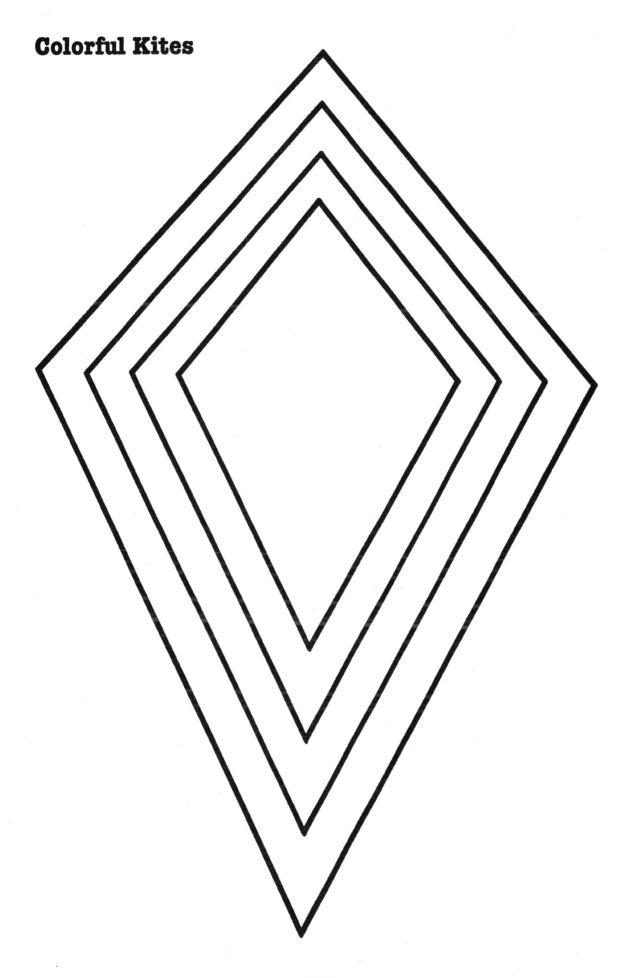

# Fingerpaint Rainbows

## Materials and Supplies

Sheets of pre-drawn rainbows (See illustration on the next page.)

Different colors of fingerpaints in shallow containers (For each tray fold a paper towel in quarters. Lay it in the tray. Pour the paint over each towel.)

Paper towels

## Activity

Set the supplies on the table.

Have each child take a rainbow. Show them how to dip their index fingers into one color of fingerpaint and paint along one line of the rainbow. Encourage them to re-dip their fingers when they need more paint. When that color is complete, have them wipe the paint off their fingers, choose a different color and paint the next line. Continue until all the lines on the rainbow are painted.

### Play Again – It's Fun!

*Classroom Rainbow:* Draw a large rainbow. On the first day put out one color of fingerpaint. Have the children use that color to make fingerpaint dots along one of the lines. On the second day, make fingerpaint dots with a different color along the second line. Continue until the rainbow is full of color.

On ST. PATRICK'S DAY add a pot of gold to the end of the rainbow.

# Fingerpaint Rainbows

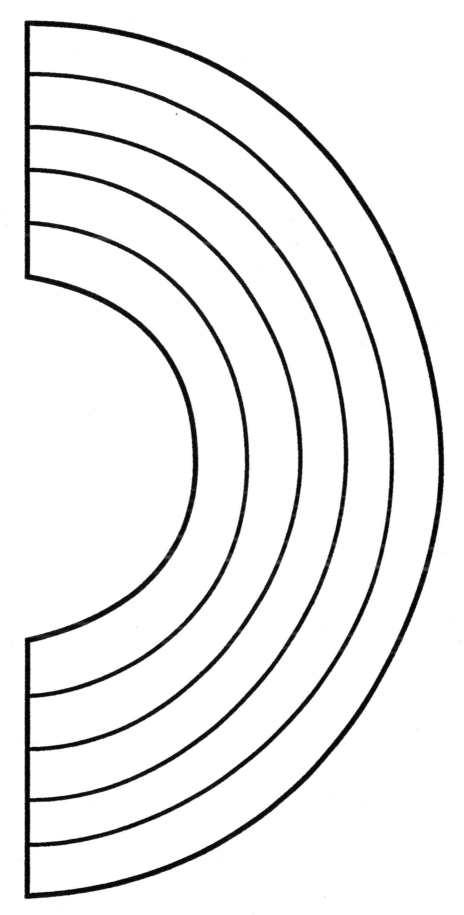

# Catch a Floating Cloud

## Themes

Clouds
Weather
Wind and Air

## Use With

Individuals
Small Groups

## Skills

Eye-Hand
  Coordination
Visual Motor
  Control
Control of
  Facial Muscles
Cooperation
Play Together

## Materials and Supplies

Facial tissues such as Kleenex®

## Activity

Play CATCH A FLOATING CLOUD in a large open area.

Give each player a tissue. Have them tilt their heads back and hold the tissues in both hands about 6" from their mouths. Blow the tissues up in the air. As the "clouds" float down, encourage the children to catch them.

### Play Again – It's Fun!

*Pair Up:* One child blows her "cloud" in the air and her partner catches it.

# Picking Flowers

## Themes

Flowers

Spring

Summer

## Use With

Individuals

Small Groups

## Skills

Visual Motor Control

Eye-Hand Coordination

Upper Body Control

## Materials and Supplies

Lots of artificial flowers (6" stems make it easier for children to pick up)

Small unbreakable vases or baskets

4-5 large pieces of black construction paper

## Activity

Cut large black ovals from construction paper. Pretend they are patches of "dirt." Tape the "dirt" to the floor, leave room around each one.

Have the children sit crossed-legged on the patches of "dirt." Give each player a vase/basket. Have them hold their vases/baskets in their non-dominant hands. Scatter the flowers all around the "dirt," but within the players reach.

When you say, *"Start picking the flowers"* have the children pick up the flowers one at a time and put them in their vases/baskets. Encourage them to remain sitting on the "dirt," twisting and turning at their waists to "pick" the flowers.

# Flower Power

## Themes

Flowers
Colors
Summer
Spring

## Use With

Individuals
Small Groups

## Skills

Visual Control
Eye-Hand
 Coordination
Finger
 Coordination

## Materials and Supplies

Unsharpened pencils with erasers

Very shallow paint in flat containers such as produce trays (Could put a folded paper towel in each flat container and then pour different colors of paint over them or use different colored ink pads.)

One or more flower shapes (See next page.)

## Activity

Set the paint trays on the table with one or two pencils for each color. Let the children each pick flowers they would like to color.
Show them how to dip and re-dip the eraser end of the pencils in paint and dot the insides of their flowers with color/s.

180

**Flower Power**

# Flight of the Honey Bees

## Themes

Bees

Bugs and
  Insects

Spring

Summer

## Use With

Individuals

## Skills

Visual Motor
Control

Body
  Coordination

## Materials and Supplies

Several 4'x5' pieces of butcher paper or newsprint

Crayons, markers, or colored chalk

## Activity

Draw a tree, approximately 3' tall in the middle of the paper. Draw a bee hive in the bottom left corner, and 4-5 flowers on the right side of the tree. Attach the picture to the wall with the bottom edge touching the floor. (Repeat for each picture.)

Encourage children to pretend they are honey bees. When a child wants to play, give him a crayon, marker, or chalk and have him squat in front of the tree and put his crayon on the hive to take off. Let him mark the FLIGHT OF THE HONEY BEE by drawing a continuous line from the hive, up and over the tree, and down to a flower. Then return home by "flying" back over the tree to the hive.

Encourage each child to make several "flights" using different colored crayons. When the bees have visited all the flowers on the sheet several times, take that sheet off the wall and attach a new one.

**Flight of the Honey Bees**

# Tree Climbing

## Materials and Supplies

Brown and green butcher paper

Colored construction paper

### Make Your CLIMBING TREES

1. Cut 3 different sized, brown tree trucks. (1'x5' – 2'x5' – 2½'x5')

2. Cut 3, green treetops, one to fit on the top of each trunk.

3. Tape the trees to a large empty wall.

4. Cut out lots of pairs of construction paper hands.

5. Glue the pairs of hands on the trunks in a particular pattern. (See pages 186-187) For example:

    - 2'x5' – glue pairs of hands

    - 2½'x5' – glue pairs of hands which alternate in and out

    - 1'x5' – glue hands which alternate right over left

## Activity

Have the children "climb" up and then down each tree by matching their hands to the construction paper hands on the trees.

### Hint:

- For younger children cut hands that are color coded. For example, all right hands would be red and left hands would be blue.

# Tree Climbing

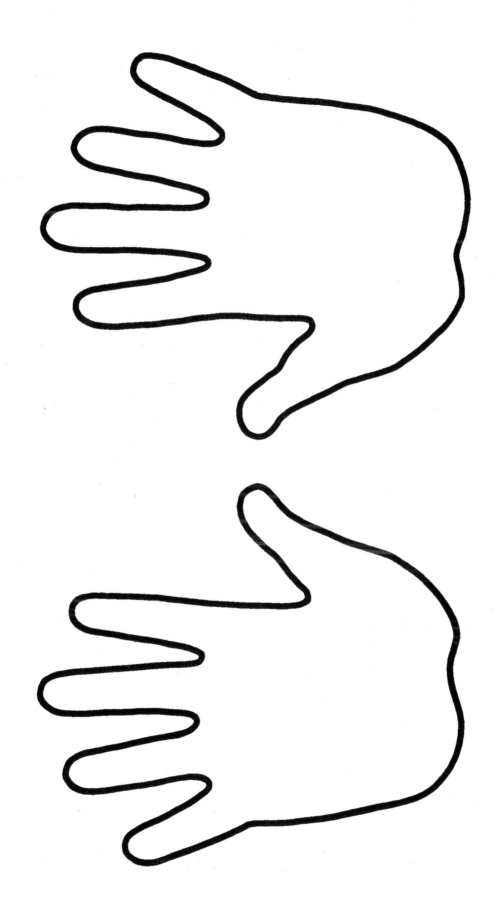

# Tree Climbing

# Tree Climbing

# Can of Worms

## Themes

Worms

Spring
  Creatures

Spring

## Use With

Individuals

## Skills

Eye-Hand
  Coordination

Finger
  Coordination

Count Objects

## Materials and Supplies

Heavy weight yarn

3 pound coffee can with plastic lid

Tweezers with rounded tips

### Make Your CAN OF WORMS

1. Cut 10-15, 24" pieces of yarn for each CAN OF WORMS.

2. Punch 10-15 holes in each plastic coffee can lid.

3. Push one piece of yarn through each hole. Tie a large knot in each end of each piece of yarn.

4. Pull all the pieces of yarn through the bottom of each lid. Only the top knots are visible. Put the lid on the coffee can. All the WORMS are hiding inside the can.

5. Repeat for each CAN OF WORMS.

## Activity

Have several unbreakable trays. Set one CAN OF WORMS and a pair of tweezers on each tray.

Have the children pull out each worm by grabbing a knot with the tweezers and pulling it the full length of the yarn. Encourage the children to count the worms as they pull them out.

### Play Again – It's Fun!

*Pull With Tongs:* Use pairs of small tongs to pull each worm.

*Pull With Fingers:* Use your thumb and index finger to pull each worm.

# Fat Worms

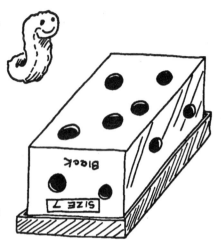

## Themes

Worms

Spring
Creatures

Rain

Spring and
Summer

## Use With

Individuals

Small Groups

## Skills

Finger
Coordination

Eye-Hand
Coordination

## Materials and Supplies

Styrofoam packing peanuts

Several shoe boxes

### Make Your WORMS and THEIR HOUSES

1. WORMS – Draw eyes on the styrofoam peanuts with permanent markers.

2. WORM HOUSES – Turn shoe boxes upside down.

3. Punch several large holes in the bottoms and sides of the shoe boxes.

4. Put the lids back on the shoe boxes.

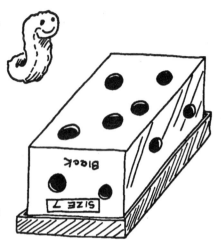

## Activity

Set the WORM HOUSES, lids down, on large trays. Lay the "worms" on the tray around the box. Put the trays on a table. Have the children wiggle their "worms" home and put them, head first, through the holes.

# Wiggle Worms

## Materials and Supplies

Lots of brown pipe cleaners

Empty spice containers with holes or grated cheese
containers

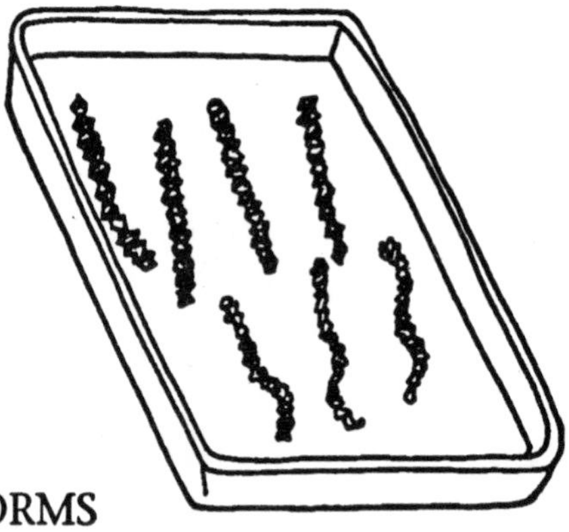

### Make Your WORMS

1. Cut the brown pipe
   cleaners into thirds.
   Put them on a large
   produce tray.

2. If you don't have all
   brown pipe cleaners,
   make COLORFUL WORMS
   by using all colors of pipe cleaners.

## Activity

Put the "worms" and spice/cheese containers on
trays. Set them on the table or floor. Have the
children put the WIGGLE WORMS through the holes
of the containers, one at a time, until all the
"worms" are gone. Empty the container and play
again.

### Play Again – It's Fun!

*More Worms:* Cut the pipe cleaners into different
length "worms." Play as above.

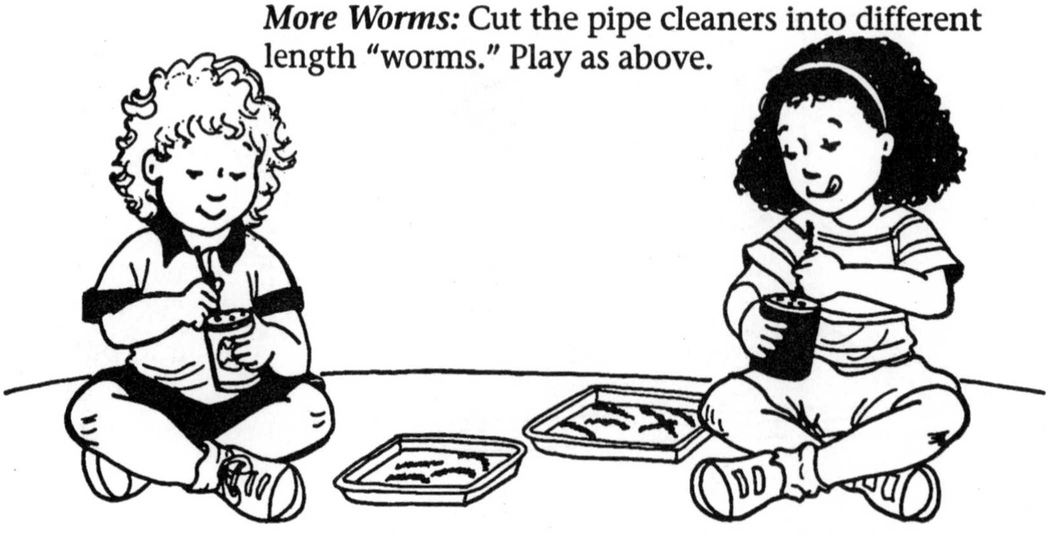

# Leap Frog

## Themes

Frogs

Ponds and
  Puddles

Spring

## Use With

Individuals

Small Groups

## Skills

Motor Planning

Body
  Coordination

Play Together

## Materials and Supplies

Green Contact® paper

Empty shoe boxes or small pillows (green if possible)

## Activity

Play LEAP FROG several different ways:

- Cut lily-pads out of Contact® paper and stick them to the floor approximately two feet apart. Have the children leap from lily pad to lily pad. Encourage the children to squat low each time they leap.

- Place shoe boxes on the floor in a row approximately two feet apart. Have the children LEAP FROG over the boxes one at a time. (Another time use pillows or shoe box lids instead of shoe boxes.)

# Picnic Ants

## Themes

Ants

Bugs and
 Insects

Summer

## Use With

Individuals

Small Groups

## Skills

Finger
 Coordination

Eye-Hand
 Coordination

## Materials and Supplies

Black stamp pads with washable ink

Picnic pages – Copy the sample on the next page or
 create your own

## Activity

When the children want to play, give them picnic
scenes and stamp pads. Have them make "ants at the
picnic" by pressing their thumb onto the stamp pad
and then onto the picnic scene, then pressing their
index finger on the pad and printing more ants onto
the picnic scene. Continue in this manner until each
fingertip has made at least one "ant."

Encourage the children to print as many "ants" as
each would like. If necessary, remind them to start
with their thumbs and end with their small fingers.
Some children might want to add detail to their ants
when they have finished printing.

**Hint:**

* Have younger children use whichever fingertips
  they'd like to.

194

# Mosquito Swat

## Themes

Bugs and Insects

Summer

## Use With

Pairs of Children

Small Groups

## Skills

Visual Motor Control

Eye-Hand Coordination

Body Awareness

Cooperation

Taking Turns

## Materials and Supplies

Flashlights

## Activity

Have the children work in pairs. Each pair stands facing each other. Give one child in each pair a flashlight.

Have the child with the flashlight shine it (representing the mosquito) somewhere on the front of the other child's body (shoulder, arm, knee, foot, etc.). The other child "swats" the mosquito. The child with the flashlight shines the light on another spot and his partner "swats" again. Encourage the children to take turns shining the light as they play MOSQUITO SWAT.

# Finding Fireflies

## Materials and Supplies

Wide yellow fluorescent highlighter markers

Large sheets of 3'x5' blue paper

Several flashlights or pen lights

## Activity

Attach the paper to the wall approximately 6" from the floor. Have the flashlights and highlighter markers in a bucket. Place it on the floor near the paper.

Have the children work in pairs, one holding the flashlight (firefly) and the other holding the marker.

Have the child with the "firefly" fly it someplace on the paper and land. Have the child with the marker quickly find the "firefly" and mark the spot before he flies away.

Have the children take turns. When they are finished, encourage them to add wings and details to their "fireflies."

# Sack of Snakes

## Themes

Zoo Animals

Crawling
Creatures

Snakes

## Use With

Individuals

Small Groups

## Skills

Hand Strength

Eye-Hand
Coordination

Imagination

## Materials and Supplies

Lots of 4"x14" strips of brown butcher paper or
grocery bag paper

Lunch bags

## Activity

Place the strips of paper in the middle of the table.
Have each child make as many "snakes" as she would
like by crumpling each strip of paper along the entire
length and then twisting it until it's tight.

Have paint, markers, crayons, etc. on the table. Let
the children add detail to their "snakes." When dry,
encourage the children to crawl the "snakes" into
their homes (lunch bags). Let the children take their
SACKS OF SNAKES home and show them to their
families.

# Sun Catchers

## Themes

Weather
Summer
Sky

## Use With

Individuals
Small Groups

## Skills

Hand Strength
Eye-Hand
  Coordination

## Materials and Supplies

White glue slightly thinned with water

Glue brushes

Hole punchers

Variety of colors of construction paper, discarded
  greeting cards, etc.

Clear plastic lids from coffee cans, yogurt containers,
  margarine tubs, etc.

## Activity

Have the supplies and materials on the table.

When a child wants to make a SUN CATCHER, first
let him brush glue on the bottom of a plastic lid.
After it is covered, let him choose a piece of paper/
card, hold it about one foot over the sticky lid, and
punch holes in it so the dots fall on the glue.
Encourage him to pick a variety of papers and cards
as he continues punching holes for as long as he
would like.

After the SUN CATCHERS have dried, string them
with pieces of colored yarn and hang them in sunny
windows.

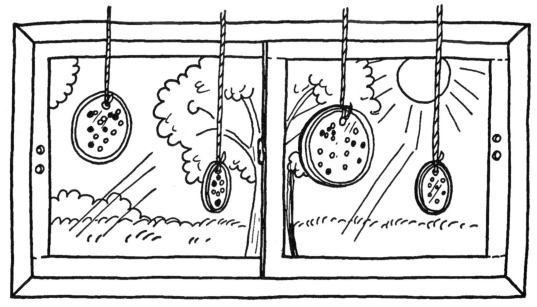

# Animal Rescue

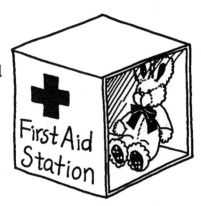

## Themes

Animals

Occupations

Body Awareness

## Use With

Small Groups

Large Groups

## Skills

Motor Planning

Body
 Coordination

Play Together

Caring for
 Others

## Materials and Supplies

Small stuffed animals such as a dog, cat, rabbit, teddy
 bear, frog, etc.

Parachute, large bed sheet, tablecloth, or blanket

Large box for a FIRST AID STATION

## Activity

Have the children sit around a parachute. Put the FIRST AID STATION just outside the circle. Pass around the animals. Tell the children that all these animals were playing on the beach and got swept into the water by a giant wave. (Have the children lift up the parachute and let the children holding the animals put them under the chute in the middle. Lower the parachute so the animals are covered.)

The children will have to rescue these animals and take them to the FIRST AID STATION. Have the children stand and hold the edge of the chute. Everyone gently move their arms up and down making ocean waves. Call out one child's name. She swims under the parachute to the animals, rescues one, and gently carries it to the FIRST AID STATION and then returns to the parachute. Continue playing until all the animals have been rescued and are safely in the FIRST AID STATION.

### Continue Playing – It's Fun!

*Care For the Animals:* Put the FIRST AID STATION in a quiet area of the room. Add veterinarian supplies to the STATION. Let the children take care of the rescued animals.

# Flash and Unclip

## Themes

Clothing

## Use With

Pairs of
  Children

## Skills

Visual Control

Finger
  Coordination

Play Together

Cooperation

## Materials and Supplies

Small bucket

Flashlights

8-10 spring-loaded clips with
  different length handles,
  such as:

- Butterfly clips
- Chip clips
- Office clips
- Colored clothes pins

## Activity

Put all the clips in the bucket. Have the children play
in pairs.

Encourage them to work together to attach the clips
to the front of one child's clothing. After all the clips
have been fastened, the other
child gets a flashlight and
stands facing his
partner. He shines
the light on one clip
and the child
removes it from his
clothing and puts it
back in the bucket.
The children
continue, shining
the light and
unclipping the clips
one at a time until
they are all removed.
The children change
places and play
again.

# Dot-Dot-Dot Flags

**Themes**

United States
  Holidays

Parades

**Use With**

Individuals

Small Groups

**Skills**

Eye-Hand
  Coordination

Play Together

## Materials and Supplies

Tiny sponge balls (Clip a clothes pin to each ball)

Red paint in shallow trays

Blue crayons

White paint in small shallow trays (Fold paper towels into quarters. Set one folded towel in each tray. Pour the white paint over the paper towel.)

### Make Your UNITED STATES FLAG PAGES

(Use illustration on the next page or make your own FLAG PAGES.)

1. On a sheet of white paper draw a large flag shape rectangle.

2. In the upper left hand corner, draw a small rectangle.

3. From the top to the bottom of the paper draw **12** evenly spaced horizontal lines.

4. Make at least one FLAG PAGE for each child.

## Activity

Give the children FLAG Pages. Show them how to DOT-DOT-DOT the stripes by dipping sponge balls in red paint and printing circles in every other stripe. As each child dots, encourage her to touch the previous dot.

After the DOTS have dried, let the children color the small rectangles in their FLAGS blue and then add stars by dipping and re-dipping one index finger into the white paint and dotting the blue rectangle.

### Continue Playing – It's Fun!

*Have a Parade:* Let the children glue their flags to paint stir sticks. Have a neighborhood parade.

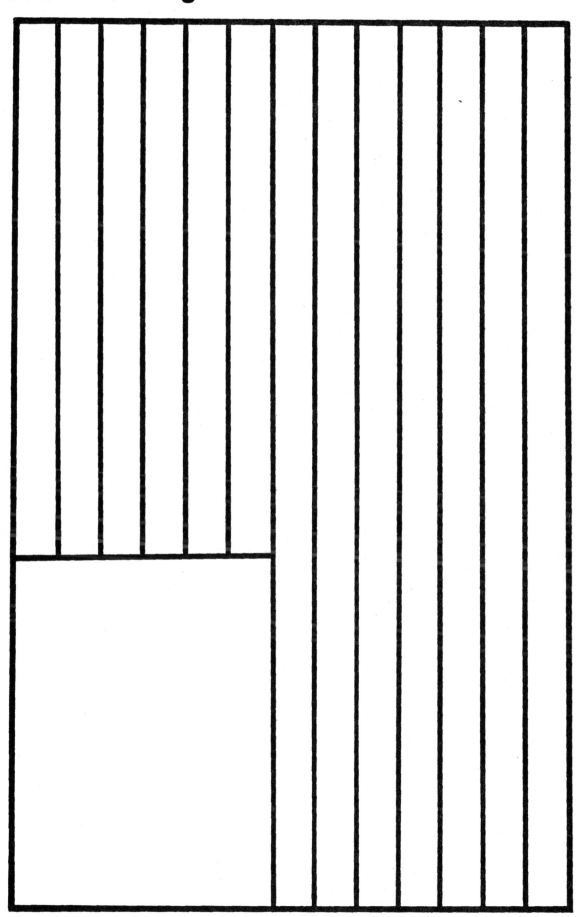

# Beginner's Baseball

## Themes

Sports

Summer

## Use With

Small Groups

Large Groups

## Skills

Hand Strength

Visual Motor
Control

Play Together

## Materials and Supplies

Paper towel tubes      $\frac{1}{2}$ sheets of newspaper

Paper bags

## Activity

Give each child a paper bag, a stack of newspaper, and a paper towel tube.

Have the children use both hands to crumple each piece of newspaper into a tight ball. Put the balls in their bags. In a large open area, have the children throw their paper balls into the air one at a time and hit them with their tubes. (Remember to stand far apart.)

After all the balls have been hit, encourage the children to gather them up and play again.

### Hints:

- Make the "balls" in the room and then hit them outside.

- Have younger children put all the balls in one container instead of individual bags.

### Play Again – It's Fun!

*Beginner's Golf:* Have children make golf balls with small sheets of newspaper. Use wrapping paper tubes for golf clubs.

# Bubble Pop

## Themes

Summer Fun

Circles

## Use With

Pairs of Children

## Skills

Eye-Hand Coordination

Visual Motor Control

Play Together

Taking Turns

## Materials and Supplies

Paper towel tubes

Bubble solution and wands

## Activity

Have the children work in pairs. One child has the bubbles and the other one has a paper towel tube in each hand. As one child blows the bubbles, the other child "pops" each bubble between his tubes. Change places and play again.

**Hint:**

* To help children maintain focus and control, have them sit in chairs facing each other as they play.

**Play Again – It's Fun!**

*Kneel and Pop:* Have both players kneel as they play. Another time sit crossed-legged and play.

# Boxes and Balls I

## Themes

Balls

Summer

## Use With

Individuals

Small Groups

## Skills

Body
  Coordination

Eye-Hand
  Coordination

Cooperation

Play Together

## Materials and Supplies

3 medium size boxes

Wide tape

Balls in a variety of sizes in a basket

## Activity

In an open, less traveled area, place the boxes in a line or a semicircle. About 3 feet from the boxes, put a tape line on the floor so children know where to stand. Set the basket of balls near the tape line.

Have the children toss the balls into the boxes. If a child misses the box, he or a friend can go get it. After all the balls have been tossed into the boxes, have the children put them back in the basket and play again.

# Boxes and Balls II

## Themes

Beanbags and Balls

Summer Fun

## Use With

Individuals

Small Groups

## Skills

Visual Motor Control

Play Together

## Materials and Supplies

5-10 assorted sizes of boxes

Items to throw, such as:

Foam balls

Beanbags

Small beach balls

Crumpled paper balls

Sock balls

Tennis balls

## Activity

In an open area, put all the boxes together with their sides touching.

Have one or more children sit around the boxes. Give each player a variety of things to throw. Encourage them to throw the items into different boxes. As the children continue to play, make the game more challenging by having the children sit further away from the boxes.

# Box Exchange

## Themes

Body
  Movements

## Use With

Small Groups

Large Groups

## Skills

Motor Planning

Body
  Coordination

Play Together

## Materials and Supplies

1 large box, with the tops cut off, for each child (big enough for a child to stand in)

## Activity

In a large open area, scatter the boxes with the open end up.

Tell the children that they are going to play BOX EXCHANGE. To start, have each child choose a box and stand in it. You will call out a movement and then say *"Box Exchange!"* They should pick a different box, move to it the way you directed, and then stand inside that box. If another child gets there first, the second child should just choose another box. When all the children are in their new boxes you will call out another movement and play again.

For example:

- *"Hop – Box Exchange."*
- *"Crawl – Box Exchange."*
- *"Twirl – Box Exchange."*

# Hoop Bounce

### Themes

Summer Fun

Balls

### Use With

Small Groups

### Skills

Body
  Coordination

Visual Control

Play Together

## Materials and Supplies

Hula hoops

Playground balls

## Activity

Have the children work with partners. Put a hula hoop/s on the ground. Have 2 children stand on either side of the hoop. Give one child a ball. She bounces it in the hoop to her partner who catches it and bounces it back. Continue playing.

# Barefoot Walk

## Themes

Senses

Body Awareness

## Use With

Individuals

Small Groups

## Skills

Motor Planning

Tactile
  Awareness

Play Together

## Materials and Supplies

20' piece of canvas or stiff fabric

8" - 10" squares of a variety of textures, such as:

  Felt

  Foam

  Carpet

  Sandpaper

  Corrugated cardboard

  Fur

  Contact paper® sticky side up

  Satin

  Velvet

  Terry cloth

  Rubber tread

  Vinyl

  Sponge

  Burlap

# Activity

Make your BAREFOOT WALK by gluing pieces of the above textures to the long strip of canvas or sturdy fabric. Leave about 8" between each texture.

Lay the BAREFOOT SIDEWALK in an open area. Have the children take off their shoes and socks. Let them slowly walk the path, exploring each texture with their toes. Encourage them to talk about how each texture feels: soft, hard, rough, tickly, etc.

After the children have explored the BAREFOOT WALK, encourage them to walk along it in different ways, such as sideways, tip-toe, to music, etc.

**Hint:**

- When finished, fold up the BAREFOOT WALK in an accordion fold and store for another time.

# Connect the "Dots"

## Themes

Shapes
Summer Fun

## Use With

Small Groups

## Skills

Visual Motor
Control

Body
Coordination

Play Together

Identify Shapes

## Materials and Supplies

Sidewalk chalk

## Activity

On a large sidewalk or blacktop area, mark off a large square, at least 10'x10'.

Give one child the piece of chalk. Have 6-8 children stand somewhere within the 10' space. They are the "dots." The child with the chalk CONNECTS THE "DOTS" by drawing a straight line from child to child. After all the "dots" are connected, the children should step back and look at the shape/design. Talk about what they see in the shape/design.

### Play Again – It's Fun!

*More Connect the Dots:* Have the children stand in different places. CONNECT THE "DOTS" with different colors of sidewalk chalk.

*Color Your Dot:* After the "dots" have been connected, let the children decorate their spots with different colors of chalk.

# Shooting Stars

## Themes

Summer

Weather

Sky

## Use With

Individuals

Small Groups

Large Groups

## Skills

Breath Control

Visual Motor
  Control

Play Together

Cooperation

## Materials and Supplies

Cotton balls

Straws

Blue posterboard or large sheet of butcher paper

Waste basket

## Activity

Lay the large sheet of blue paper on the floor and tape it down. Spread lots of cotton balls on the floor near the edges of the paper. Have several containers of straws.

Encourage the children to lie on the floor and blow the stars into the sky or pick them up in their straws and drop them in the sky. The next day, let the children use glue sticks to glue all the SHOOTING STARS in the sky. Add gummed stars to make the sky even more brilliant! Hang for everyone to see.

### Play Again – It's Fun!

*Summer Fireworks:* Dip ping pong balls in different colors of poster paint, lay them on the edge of black/blue paper. Have the children blow the balls across the paper making COLORFUL FIREWORKS. Talk about fireworks the children have seen as they are playing.

# Theme & Holiday Index

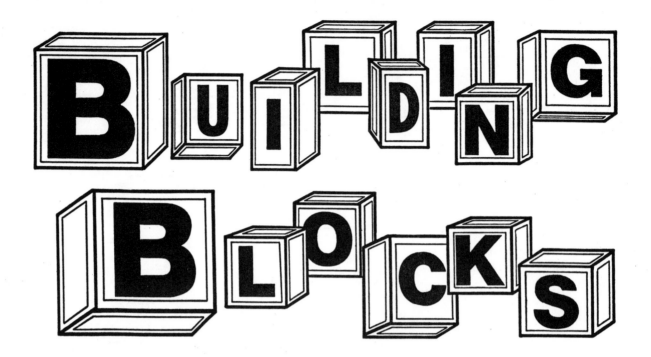

# Building Blocks Library

## The Circle Time Series

*by Liz and Dick Wilmes.* Hundreds of activities for large and small groups of children. Each book is filled with Language and Active games, Fingerplays, Songs, Stories, Snacks, and more. A great resource for every library shelf.

### Circle Time Book
Captures the spirit of 39 holidays and seasons.
**ISBN 0-943452-00-7** $ 12.95

### Everyday Circle Times
Over 900 ideas. Choose from 48 topics divided into 7 sections: self-concept, basic concepts, animals, foods, science, occupations, and recreation.
**ISBN 0-943452-01-5** $16.95

### More Everyday Circle Times
Divided into the same 7 sections as EVERYDAY. Features new topics such as Birds and Pizza, plus all new ideas for some popular topics contained in EVERYDAY.
**ISBN 0-943452-14-7** $16.95

### Yearful of Circle Times
52 different topics to use weekly, by seasons, or mixed throughout the year. New Friends, Signs of Fall, Snowfolk Fun, and much more.
**ISBN 0-943452-10-4** $16.95

C I R C L E   T I M E

## Paint Without Brushes

*by Liz and Dick Wilmes.* Use common materials which you already have. Discover the painting possibilities in your classroom! PAINT WITHOUT BRUSHES gives your children open-ended art activities to explore paint in lots of creative ways. A valuable art resource. One you'll want to use daily.
**ISBN 0-943452-15-5** $12.95

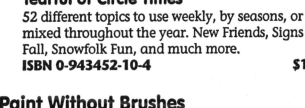

## Easel Art

*by Liz & Dick Wilmes.* Let the children use easels, walls, outside fences, clip boards, and more as they enjoy the variety of art activities filling the pages of EASEL ART. A great book to expand young children's art experiences.
**ISBN 0-943452-25-2** $ 12.95

## Everyday Bulletin Boards

*by Wilmes and Moehling.* Features borders, murals, backgrounds, and other open-ended art to display on your bulletin boards. Plus board ideas with patterns, which teachers can make and use to enhance their curriculum.
**ISBN 0-943452-09-0** $ 12.95

## Exploring Art

*by Liz and Dick Wilmes.* EXPLORING ART is divided by months. Over 250 art ideas for paint, chalk, doughs, scissors, and more. Easy to set-up in your classroom.
**ISBN 0-943452-05-8** $19.95

A R T

## Magnet Board Fun

*by Liz and Dick Wilmes.* Every classroom has a magnet board, every home a refrigerator. MAGNET BOARD FUN is crammed full of games, songs, and stories. Hundreds of patterns to reproduce, color, and use immediately.
**ISBN 0-943452-28-7**                    **$16.95**

## Parachute Play

*by Liz and Dick Wilmes.* Play year 'round. Starting with basic techniques, PARACHUTE PLAY provides over 100 activities to use with your parachute.
**ISBN 0-943452-03-1**                    **$ 9.95**

## Activities Unlimited

*by Adler, Caton, and Cleveland.* Hundreds of innovative activities to help children develop fine and gross motor skills, increase language, become self-reliant, and play cooperatively. This book will quickly be a favorite.
**ISBN 0-943452-17-1**                    **$16.95**

## Felt Board Fingerplays

*by Liz and Dick Wilmes.*  A year full of fingerplay fun. Over 50 popular fingerplays, with full-size patterns. All accompanied by games and activities.
**ISBN 0-943452-26-0**                    **$16.95**

## Felt Board Fun

*by Liz and Dick Wilmes.* Make your felt board come alive. This unique book has over 150 ideas with patterns.
**ISBN 0-943452-02-3**                    **$16.95**

## Table & Floor Games

*by Liz and Dick Wilmes.* 32 easy-to-make, fun-to-play table/floor games with accompanying patterns ready to trace or photocopy. Teach beginning concepts such as matching, counting, colors, alphabet, sorting and so on.
**ISBN 0-943452-16-3**                    **$19.95**

## Learning Centers

*by Liz and Dick Wilmes.* Hundreds of open-ended activities to quickly involve and excite your children. You'll use it every time you plan and whenever you need a quick, additional activity. A must for every teacher's bookshelf.
**ISBN 0-943452-13-9**                    **$19.95**

## Play With Big Boxes

*by Liz and Dick Wilmes.* Children love big boxes. Turn them into boats, telephone booths, tents, and other play areas. Bring them to art and let children collage, build, and paint them. Use them in learning centers for games, play stages, quiet spaces, puzzles, and more, more, more.
**ISBN 0-943452-23-6**                    **$ 12.95**

## Play With Small Boxes

*by Liz and Dick Wilmes.* Small boxes are free, fun, and provide unlimited possibilities. Use them for telephones, skates, scoops, pails, beds, buggies, and more. So many easy activities, you'll want to use small boxes every day.
**ISBN 0-943452-24-4**                    **$ 12.95**

## Games for All Seasons

*by Caton and Cleveland.* Play with the wonder of seasons and holidays. Use acorns, pumpkins, be clouds and butterflies, go ice fishing. Over 150 learning games.
**ISBN 0-943452-29-5**                    **$ 16.95**

# 2's Experience Series

*by Liz and Dick Wilmes.* An exciting series developed especially for toddlers and twos!

## 2's-Art
Scribble, Paint, Smear, Mix, Tear, Mold, Taste, and more. Over 150 activities, plus lots of recipes and hints.

**ISBN 0-943452-21-X**

**$16.95**

## 2's-Sensory Play
Hundreds of playful, multi-sensory activities to encourage children to look, listen, taste, touch, and smell.

**ISBN 0-943452-22-8**

**$14.95**

## 2's-Dramatic Play
Dress up and pretend! Hundreds of imaginary characters...

**ISBN 0-943452-20-1**

**$12.95**

## 2's-Stories
Excite children with story books! Read— expand the stories with games, songs, and rhymes. Over 40 books with patterns.

**ISBN 0-943452-27-9**

**$16.95**

## 2's-Fingerplays
A wonderful collection of easy fingerplays with accompanying games and large FINGERPLAY CARDS.

**ISBN 0-943452-18-X**

**$12.95**

## 2's-Felt Board Fun
Make your felt board come alive. Enjoy stories, activities, and rhymes. Hundreds of extra large patterns.

**ISBN 0-943452-19-8**

**$14.95**

| | |
|---|---|
| **BUILDING BLOCKS Subscription** | **$ 20.00** |
| **2's EXPERIENCE Series** | |
| 2'S EXPERIENCE - ART | 16.95 |
| 2'S EXPERIENCE - DRAMATIC PLAY | 12.95 |
| 2'S EXPERIENCE - FELTBOARD FUN | 14.95 |
| 2'S EXPERIENCE - FINGERPLAYS | 12.95 |
| 2'S EXPERIENCE - SENSORY PLAY | 14.95 |
| 2'S EXPERIENCE - STORIES | 16.95 |
| **CIRCLE TIME Series** | |
| CIRCLE TIME BOOK | 12.95 |
| EVERYDAY CIRCLE TIMES | 16.95 |
| MORE EVERYDAY CIRCLE TIMES | 16.95 |
| YEARFUL OF CIRCLE TIMES | 16.95 |
| **ART** | |
| EASEL ART | 12.95 |
| EVERYDAY BULLETIN BOARDS | 12.95 |
| EXPLORING ART | 19.95 |
| PAINT WITHOUT BRUSHES | 12.95 |
| **LEARNING GAMES & ACTIVITIES** | |
| ACTIVITIES UNLIMITED | 16.95 |
| FELT BOARD FINGERPLAYS | 16.95 |
| FELT BOARD FUN | 16.95 |
| GAMES FOR ALL SEASONS | 16.95 |
| LEARNING CENTERS | 19.95 |
| MAGNET BOARD FUN | 16.95 |
| PARACHUTE PLAY | 9.95 |
| PLAY WITH BIG BOXES | 12.95 |
| PLAY WITH SMALL BOXES | 12.95 |
| TABLE & FLOOR GAMES | 19.95 |

Prices subject to change without notice.

*All books available from full-service book stores, educational stores, and school supply catalogs.*

Check Our Website:
www.bblockspubl.com

---

# TODDLERS & TWO'S